PAINT

AND COLOR IN DECORATION

PAINT

AND COLOR IN DECORATION

FARROW&BALL

First published in the United States of America
in 2003
Rizzoli International Publications, Inc.
300 Park Avenue South
New York, NY 10010
www.rizzoliusa.com

First published in Great Britain in 2003 by Cassell
Illustrated, a division of Octopus Publishing Group
Limited, 2–4 Heron Quays, London E14 4JP

Copyright © 2003 Farrow & Ball Limited

Text: Joseph Friedman
Editors: Farrow & Ball
Photography: Ivan Terestchenko with the
exception of page 22 (top: © Royal Academy of
Arts, bottom: © Alex Starkey/Country Life Picture
Library), page 26 (both images reproduced by
permission of Sir John Soane's Museum) and page
182 (© National Trust Photographic Library/John
Hammond)

All rights reserved. No part of this publication may
be reproduced, stored in a retrieval system, or
transmitted in any form or by any means,
electronic, mechanical, photocopying, recording, or
otherwise, without prior consent of the publishers.

2003 2004 2005 2006 2007/ 10 9 8 7 6 5 4 3 2 1

Printed in Italy by L.E.G.O.

ISBN: 0-8478-2593-0

Library of Congress Catalog Control Number:
2003108547

Page 2: Boughton White. Boughton is a house that slept for two hundred years. Originally built in the late seventeenth century, soon afterwards it ceased to play any major role in the life of its owners and was not fully revived until the early years of the twentieth century. The result is that the interior retains a wealth of historic detail undisturbed by changing fashion, including this paneled lobby, which still preserves an early off-white scheme in traditional lead paint.

Opposite: Tapestry Drawing Room, Goodwood. The ceiling retains its original painted decoration in a range of colors that were carefully selected by the architect James Wyatt to tone with the magnificent wall hangings depicting scenes from the story of Don Quixote.

Front Cover & This Page: Detail of the paintwork in the Breakfast Room at Calke Abbey, Derbyshire.

CONTENTS

THE ART OF THE DECORATOR

Color means more to me than any of my other raw materials. I get infinite pleasure from color—experimenting with it and exploiting it. Most people are afraid of color... It is one of the most exciting, rewarding and inexpensive things, and can easily create a complete transformation in any room.

—David Hicks

This book celebrates the work of those designers who, through the medium of paint, have created some of the world's most beautiful and influential interiors. For us, as paint makers, these designers have been a particular inspiration, and a constant source of ideas and information, not only in providing specific colors and facts about materials and techniques, but in fashioning our whole approach or philosophy. This book is a personal tribute to their achievements, but also, we hope, a means of sharing with others the lessons and, above all, the pleasures we have drawn from them.

Not all of the designers we feature were interior decorators; some worked at a time when the very concept of the interior decorator was unknown. But all were directly involved in the decoration of interiors, all used paint as one of the principal components of their work, and all were masters of that medium, leaving a rich legacy of interiors and designs that continue to provide inspiration today. Some, in fact, are still at work, constantly expanding and enriching the tradition of painted decoration while pointing ways forward to the future.

Our aim has been to show the broadest possible range of colors and color combinations, but also to explore the materials and techniques that lie behind them so as to provide an insight into the working methods of designers, as well as their achievements. Color in paint is dependent in the first place on pigment, but it is not just the type of pigment that counts, but the level. Many

modern paints contain up to 30 percent less pigment than traditional paints, and this of course reduces the "depth" of color produced. No less important is the liquid medium or "vehicle" with which the pigment is mixed. The identical pigment mixed with two different blends of oil paint will produce two different colors; and other colors again will result if the pigment is mixed with distemper or limewash or emulsion. Equally, the "finish," or final coat, can produce a change of color. A "flatted," or matte, finish, achieved through the use of oil of turpentine, will produce one color, and a varnished or glazed finish quite another. Even the method by which the paint is applied can have an influence. Everyone will be aware that particular types of brushes or rollers produce a particular surface, which in turn produces a particular color. An understanding of the ways in which all these various factors combine to produce particular effects is central to the art of decorating with paint, and again we have aimed to show as wide a range of these effects as possible.

Our specific focus is Great Britain and Ireland, but it is important to realize the influence of foreign design, and the fact that some of the interiors we feature were created both for and by individuals from abroad. We have also chosen examples which, however early in date, are directly relevant to mainstream decorating practice today and can generally be reproduced by the amateur as well as the professional. To look at painted decoration in all its forms would involve

Opposite: Buckram Yellow. The use of buckram as a covering for the walls of the Dining Room at Barons Court (pages 134–5) shows the influence that surface can have on color in painted decoration, which, as decorator David Hicks well understood, is never a simple matter of paint or technique.

mural painting and gilding, as well as graining, marbling, japanning and other forms of illusionistic finish. Here we are concerned with the more widespread technique of painting walls, ceilings and joinery in a single color or a concentrated range of colors, a technique that, however modern, can be traced back to the very origins of painted decoration.

As far as possible, we have aimed to illustrate the achievements of designers using authentic surviving examples of their work, although this is not as simple as it sounds. Paint is subject to sometimes rapid changes through exposure to light and the atmosphere. This is especially true of early paints, which were often less stable than their modern equivalents. The march of fashion, and the relative ease and economy of renewing or replacing old paintwork mean that it is rare to find a painted interior in its original condition even after a few years. To find an interior such as the Dining Room at Dunany, Ireland (pages 12–3, 82–3), whose Pompeian red decoration is virtually untouched since the early 19th century, is close to miraculous. For this reason a bias will be found towards interiors of more recent date, principally of the 20th century.

This book is in no way intended as a history of color, but it is important to realize that designers have never operated within a vacuum. However original their contribution, all owe a debt to the past. However creative, all work within the conditions imposed by the times in which they live. This becomes obvious when one realizes that before a certain date some colors were simply unavailable. In the case of blue, for instance, it was not until the early 18th century, with the discovery of Prussian blue, that a bright blue pigment was found that was economical enough to manufacture in the sort of quantities required for painting interiors. Before this time painters had had to rely on a variety of highly costly alternatives, such as azurite, blue verditer, smalt, and ultramarine, the latter manufactured from lapis lazuli and described by one 17th-century commentator as "so vastly dear that 'tis not to be used except in pieces of great price." To the extent that bright blues were used at all in decoration, they were generally employed only sparingly, as a means of enrichment, and remained the preserve of the very rich, being found, for instance, on the ceiling of Cardinal Wolsey's Closet at Hampton Court, an interior of the 16th century, and on the ceiling of the Privy Gallery at Somerset House, decorated for Anne of Denmark in the early 17th century. Only very exceptionally was bright blue used to decorate a large area; so that when, in around 1630, the Earl of Dysart gave orders for the walls of his Dining Room at Ham House to be painted from floor to ceiling in "fair blew," using blue verditer as the pigment, he was sending the message that he was not only a very great patron but also immensely rich. For those of more limited means, the only affordable substitute was indigo, a dye extracted from plant leaves, but this produced only a muted blue, so that when Prussian blue made its appearance, this economical chemical compound, first invented by a Berlin color maker in the first decade of the 18th century, caused a sensation. At the same time also, of course, Prussian blue could be mixed with other pigments to produce brighter versions of different colors; and in time other cheap alternatives were discovered, notably artificial ultramarine, introduced in the late 1820s.

Similar developments took place in the production of green-colored paint, where, before the 18th century, designers were again faced with technical problems. Verdigris and green verditer were commonly used, but the expense once more could be a deterrent, and paint made from these pigments was often confined to details rather than large surfaces,

Opposite: At Boughton House in Northamptonshire it is possible to study historic paintwork in an outstanding state of preservation. This section of paneling retains an early scheme of traditional lead paint in "drab," a color popular in the 1690s, when Boughton was first built and decorated. Despite its density, lead paint was quite transparent, so that several coats were required. At the same time it made the paint quite heavy, so that brushwork could not easily be smoothed away. Despite the passing of time, the original "ropy" finish is still visible, while cleaning and wear and tear have made more obvious the use of multiple successive coats.

which were mostly decorated with the olives and drabs one sees so often in the background to 17th- and 18th-century portraits, and which could be produced from cheaper alternatives. It was only in the 1760s that two German brothers in Brunswick first developed a copper compound, Brunswick green, from which a strong, bright green paint could be manufactured at reasonable expense. This was followed by the discovery of other pigments of this type, such as Scheele's green, the invention of a Swedish chemist of that name in the 1770s, and emerald green, first developed and marketed in Germany in the early 19th century. Chrome yellow Brunswick green, a mixture of chrome yellow and Prussian blue, was discovered about the same period.

Chrome yellow was itself a new discovery, providing a solution to another problem that had long dogged the housepainter, namely that of producing a strong bright yellow that was both stable and affordable. Yellow paint could be produced from earth pigments, such as yellow ochre and raw sienna, which were stable and affordable but of only limited brightness. Yellows could also be produced using pigments prepared from organic dyestuffs, such as yellow berries and quercitron bark; but though bright in color they were unstable and faded rapidly. Brightness combined with stability could be produced using orpiment or lead-tin yellow, but these had other drawbacks, the former being highly toxic, the latter somewhat pale. By the second half of the 18th century two new pigments, known respectively as Naples yellow and patent yellow, had been developed that seemed to offer an answer, but it was not until the early 19th century, with the discovery of chrome yellow, that a pigment was found which not only transformed the use of yellow, but again influenced the development of related colors, including, as we have seen, chrome yellow Brunswick green.

It is clear that technology played a vitally important role in the evolution of painted decoration. The scientific breakthroughs of the 18th and early 19th centuries not only broadened the housepainter's palette, but also led to a broadening of the housepainter's role, as designers and their clients realized that through the medium of paint they could produce similar effects to those previously obtainable only through the use of fabric hangings, wallpaper and other more costly forms of decoration. In the past painted decoration had often played a subsidiary role, serving as a neutral foil or background. Now, however, it assumed a more central function, rising eventually to become, for many, the dominant element in interior decoration.

But technology was not the only force at work. Fashion, too, was a factor. Even within the relatively narrow range of colors available before the 18th century, it is clear that at different times certain colors or types of color were preferred over others. During the Restoration period, in the later 17th century, it was generally held that interiors should be painted in colors approximating to those of the materials from which they were composed. Hence the preponderance of timber-colored woodwork and bright white plaster ceilings at this time. By the 1720s, with the rise of Neo-Palladianism, a taste had developed for all-white, or predominantly white, interiors. Conversely, certain colors were never used, or only very rarely. Reds, for instance, hardly feature as a dominant paint color before the mid-18th century, even though there were stable pigments capable of producing virtually any shade of the color. It was only during the 1750s that pale reds or pinks became widespread in the decoration of English interiors, partly as a response to fashions emanating from France. Deeper, brighter reds did nor gain general acceptance until the early 19th century, when a fashion developed for

Previous Page: It is almost two hundred years since the interior of Dunany in Ireland was last redecorated, and several of the rooms retain their original "Pompeian" red paintwork dating from 1811. The color was then the height of fashion but expensive to produce, although clearly stable and hard-wearing. Many restorations of early 19th-century Pompeian red schemes exist, but this is one of only a very small number of surviving examples from the period.

these and other colors discovered amid the remains of Pompeii and Herculaneum.

Once technology had opened up the whole of the spectrum, designers were free in principle to choose whichever color they pleased. In practice, however, fashion continued to provide a measure of control. So it is, for instance, that stronger colors characterize the work of designers in the early to mid-19th century, while a taste for tertiary colors developed in the years that followed, with paler colors becoming the fashion in the late 19th and early 20th centuries. So it is again that in the 1920s and 1930s, and in the period immediately following the Second World War, traditional designers generally turned to brighter colors, while Modernists opted for whites and primary colors, just as in our own time there has been a remarkable revival of interest in historic colors, particularly those of the 18th and early 19th centuries.

Fashion also dictated that at different times particular colors were considered appropriate to particular types of room. In the 17th and early 18th centuries entrance halls and staircases were generally regarded more as an extension of the exterior of a building than as part of the interior, and so were often decorated in colors approximating to stone, with richer colors confined to the principal rooms. This idea remained strong until at least the middle of the 18th century, and still has an influence today. But by the 1770s a more liberal approach was being taken, as at Osterley Park, Middlesex, where the Vestibule and Great Staircase were painted green, or at Heveningham Hall, Suffolk, where the Staircase Hall was painted pale blue. In the early 19th century the Entrance Hall of William Beckford's house, Fonthill, in Wiltshire, was pink, while that at Sir John Soane's house in Lincoln's Inn Fields was painted in imitation of porphyry and other marbles. Conversely, there are colors

that at particular times were considered inappropriate to certain types of room. When, in the 1820s, the Duke of Wellington chose yellow for the background to his picture collection in the Waterloo Gallery at Apsley House, Piccadilly, he was roundly condemned; and it is noticeable how few yellow picture galleries there are at this period relative to those, say, in red, such as the galleries at Petworth House, Sussex, and Attingham Park, Shropshire (pages 86–89). It is not that yellow was ruled out altogether. On the contrary, the color was widely employed, being especially popular as a color for print rooms. But as a background to paintings it was not thought appropriate, although eventually ideas would change, so that in the 20th century yellow became not only acceptable but desirable in this role, as can be seen in the famous "butta-yallah" Drawing Room of designer Nancy Lancaster's house in Avery Row, London, a varnished "broken" yellow scheme of the late 1950s, and its many successors.

Just as the function of a room might determine the choice of color, so might its size and situation, and the level of exposure to natural light. Writing in the 17th century, the architect Sir Roger Pratt (1620–85) pronounced that: "The colors of a room ought not to be taken at random but to be chosen according to the much or little light, or space of the places." Over a century later the Edinburgh housepainter David Ramsay Hay echoed these remarks, recommending that rooms facing north or east should be painted in warm tones, and those facing south or west in cooler ones. Fashion dictated also that at different times particular colors were considered appropriate to the decoration of particular architectural elements. In the case of ceilings, for example, the Elizabethans considered white to be the ideal; one contemporary observer noted the "delectable

whitenesse" of ceilings at this period. In the following century Sir Roger Pratt also praised this tradition of plain "whited" ceilings. However, around the middle of the 18th century taste underwent a change, and color began to be used on the grounds of ceilings. In 1748 the Earl of Chesterfield boasted to a friend that he had had the ceiling of his "Boudoir" in London painted a "beau bleu;" and in 1752 Lady Luxborough declared her intention to have the ceiling of her bedroom in Warwickshire "painted of a color." It was clear that the monopoly of white was over, and a few years later the architect Robert Adam (1728–92) openly criticized the "glare of white, so common in every cieling, till of late," arguing that white had "always appeared to me so cold and unfinished," while color could "remove the crudeness of the white, and create a harmony between the cieling and the sidewals, with their hangings, pictures, and other decorations." Although white continued to be used, even by Adam, from this time forward one sees a high proportion of designs for ceilings with colored grounds, variously painted in blues, greens, reds and yellows. Nor were ceilings painted only in the one color, but often in several. In 1779 Elizabeth Montagu informed the Duchess of Portland that the ceilings in her house in Portman Square, London, were being painted "…in various colors according to the present fashion."

Adam's remarks are a reminder that it is not only individual colors that have changed over time, but also color combinations. Strong opinions have been voiced on this subject. As early as 1664 the architect Balthazar Gerbier (1592–1663) lambasted the decoration of the Banqueting House in Whitehall, with its "Colors placed together, which agree not one with the other, as blew & green." Another 17th-century

commentator, John Smith, published a list of the colors that, in his view, "set off best with one another…making each other look more pleasant," stating, for instance, that "*Blews* set off best with *Yellowes* and *Whites*," but "set not off with *Greens*, *Purples*, and *Browns*," and "set off [only] indifferently with *Blacks* and *Reds*." Bright color contrasts were a distinctive feature of painted decoration in the latter half of the 18th century, with pink and green often appearing together, as in the alcove of the Palm Room at Spencer House, an interior of the 1750s, and the Eating Room at Osterley Park (pages 154–5), dating from the 1770s. The Breakfast Room at Osterley was described as "lemon color, with blew ornaments," while at Newby Hall, Yorkshire, a scheme was devised with "limon color" for the walls, and the woodwork "dead white touched with pea green."

Not everyone approved of these developments. In 1786 the architect James Peacock expressed himself disgusted with the "insupportably gorgeous" effect of multi-colored ceilings, which he believed resembled nothing so much as "cheese cakes and raspberry tarts." But this was the opinion of a minority, and, if anything, color combinations grew bolder. The Regency interiors of Thomas Hope's house in Duchess Street were a blaze of contrasting color, the Drawing Room conceived in the "Saracenic" style, as Hope expresssed it, with colors "very vivid and very strongly contrasted," the walls being sky blue and the ceiling pale yellow, with traces of azure blue and sea green. Similar combinations of contrasting colors can be found at this period, as in Sir John Soane's designs for his villa, Pitzhanger, in Ealing, where the three primary colors appear together in a single room; and there are further examples of course from the later 19th and 20th centuries.

Opposite: The Tapestry Drawing Room at Goodwood, Sussex, contains what is probably the only example in England of an 18th-century colored ceiling which has never been repainted or even retouched. At the same time it has the distinction of being gilded using water-gilding, rather than oil-gilding, a technique very rarely used in architectural decoration in England. The paintwork is interesting for its finish, which shows the transparent, almost diaphanous quality of early lead paint and the "ropy," slightly oily finish, in which the movement of the painter's brush remains visibly preserved.

Writing in the 1970s, the decorator David Hicks (1929–98) confessed that he had "...always had a passion for what some people consider clashing colors. I call them vibrating colors—for instance, vermilion, shocking pink, puce, salmon pink and blue pink." However, it needs to be stressed that throughout the centuries there has existed a parallel tradition of subtle graduation and closely modulated harmony. Hicks himself was a master in this area, as can be seen in the complex yet restrained use of varying shades of off-white in the Drawing Room at Barons Court, County Tyrone (pages 66–9).

Another important aspect of painted decoration is the transition in color between adjoining interiors. Here again, fashions have changed dramatically over time. Before the mid-18th century the general practice was to paint adjoining rooms, and even whole apartments, in similar, if not identical, colors. At Montagu House, Bloomsbury, a suite of four interconnecting rooms was decorated in the late 17th century using precisely the same shade of off-white paint; and a half-century later the state apartments on the ground floor of Spencer House were painted throughout in green. The preference at this time was for visual continuity, with painted decoration providing the link; and, as one mid-18th century observer remarked, any deviation from this approach was "reckon'd absurd." However, in the second half of the 18th century, in a development that excited considerable comment at the time, the fashion took hold for decorating adjoining rooms in different colors, with the emphasis on contrast; and by the 1770s and 1780s this had become widespread, with designers producing schemes of decoration that gloried in sometimes audacious polychrome (page 22).

Just as there have been changes in the type of color used in painted decoration, so there have been changes in the type of paint. Indeed, the two developments are ultimately inseparable, for, as we have seen, the color of a paint is strictly dependent on its formulation. At various times particular formulations have enjoyed particular popularity. In the 17th century it was customary for ceilings to be painted in a soft distemper, producing a powdery, opaque finish, whereas in the 18th century oil paint was often preferred, giving a finish that was generally less matte. In the case of walls, by contrast, it was virtually automatic in the 19th century for oil paint to be used, whereas in the 20th century the use of distempers was revived. Nor was it merely the vehicle that changed—the finish too might vary. In the early 18th century a slightly shiny "ropy," or textured, surface was the norm where oil paint was used, while by the middle years of the century designers were inclining towards a "flatted" finish that was slightly smoother and more matte. In the 19th century a taste developed for glossy finishes, while in the first half of the 20th century "broken" finishes became the fashion, with scumbling, stippling, dragging, and other types of glazed top-coat decoration.

The reasons for these changes in taste are extremely complex, and obviously relate to developments in the use of color more generally, as well as fabric design, furniture and other aspects of interior decoration. Nor should one forget the influence of scientific theory and philosophy, which, though seemingly removed from the business of decoration, held considerable sway over the use of color. The nature of color and color perception are subjects that have exercised the minds of generations of scientists and philosophers, from Newton and Descartes in the 17th century, to Burke and Goethe in the 18th, as well as Schopenhauer in the 19th and even Wittgenstein in the 20th. Indeed, Wittgenstein was himself an accomplished amateur architect and designer, with strong opinions on the use of color in interior decoration, once devising a scheme combining yellow walls, black woodwork and

Opposite: Louisa Blue. The pale blue paint on the paneling in Lady Louisa Connolly's Blue Closet at Castletown dates from the 19th century and has never been renewed but simply covered over with paper hangings.

a "royal blue" carpet. Ideas that developed in learned circles were widely propagated through the publication of books and articles, and certainly penetrated the world of design. What influence they had on the humble housepainter is debatable. As one 17th-century writer confessed, color theory was "one of the abstrusest . . . subjects in Natural Philosophy." Goethe himself bemoaned the ". . . decided aversion for all theoretical views representing color and everything belonging to it . . . among painters." But the more important designers would naturally have been conversant with such issues, and there is some evidence that even the most exalted ideas filtered down through the popularizing medium of mainstream literature and even trade publications, notably David Ramsay Hay's *The Laws of Harmonious Coloring Adapted to House Painting* (1828).

What is certain is that publications such as Hay's reached a very large audience, specifically those involved in the decoration of interiors. Already in 1670 John Evelyn had devoted several pages of his widely read treatise *Sylva* to the use of color in housepainting; and in 1676 John Smith included a whole chapter on the subject in *The Art of Painting*. A revised edition of Smith's book appeared in 1687, followed by six further editions in the 18th century and two more in the 1820s, by which time several other such books had been published, including *The Painter and Varnisher's Guide* (1804) and John Pincot's *Treatise on the Practical Part of Coach and House Painting* (1811). The 19th century saw an explosion of writing and publishing in this area. In 1825, Knight and Lacey issued their *Painter's and Varnisher's Pocket Manual*, to be followed in 1827 by Nathaniel Whittock's *The Decorative Painter's and Glazier's Guide*, and in 1828 by T. H. Vanherman's *The Painter's Cabinet and Colorman's Repository*. The 1830s saw the publication of M. Taylor's *The Painter's, Gilder's, and Varnisher's Manual*, while in the

following decade there appeared the Arrowsmiths' *The House Decorator and Painter's Guide* (1840) and William Mullinger Higgins' *The House Painter or Decorator's Companion* (1841). From this time forward there was a flood of books and articles devoted to the subject of housepainting and, indeed, the wider theme of interior decoration; and the appeal and influence of these publications only increased with the growing use of color illustrations. Every designer working today knows how much he or she owes to this vitally important source of information and ideas.

Historians, too, have played their part. By preserving the memory of fashions from the past they have sometimes influenced the fashions of the present. When architect and antiquary John Goldicutt published his *Specimens of Ancient Decorations from Pompeii* in 1825, with seductive hand-colored plates, he must surely have realized that these would soon be copied, just as designer Mario Praz would have been aware that his landmark *History of Interior Decoration*, first published in 1964, was bound to contribute to the burgeoning historicism of interior decoration in his own time. The publication of John Fowler and John Cornforth's *English Decoration in the 18th Century* (1974) was another landmark, providing a wealth of detailed information about the practices as well the tastes of the Georgian period, while the work of contemporary historians such as Ian Bristow, the leading authority on the history of paint in architectural decoration and author of the definitive twin studies *Architectural Color in British Interiors 1615–1840* and *Interior House-Painting Colors and Technology 1615–1840* (1996), provides an obvious stimulus to others involved in the restoration or decoration of historic interiors.

Of the designers featured in this book, many were architects. Before the rise of the interior decorator in the 19th century, it was

Opposite: Books on color and paint. From the late 17th century a flood of books and articles appeared on the subjects of color and paint. Addressed in the main to designers and housepainters, these books had an enormous influence on the development of taste and technique in painted decoration.

generally the architect who, in consultation with the client, chose the colors for the principal rooms. Sir Roger Pratt was adamant on this point, insisting that the architect should have "his choice as to the color." Nonetheless, it was rare before the middle of the 18th century for architects to express color in their designs. Most of our knowledge about their use of color comes from other sources, such as painters' accounts, contemporary descriptions of interiors, and the analysis of surviving paintwork. One notable exception is a ravishing ceiling design, strongly tinted in blue, that Inigo Jones (1573–1652) produced for the Duke of Buckingham around 1620, and there are others of a later date, including a wall elevation by John Talman (1677–1726), showing the architect's proposed decoration of an interior, possibly at Hampton Court, with varying shades of buff-colored wash.

From the 1750s colored designs abound, among them a magnificent set of drawings prepared by the Palladian architect John Vardy (d. 1765) for the state apartments of Spencer House, including the so-called Palm Room, with walls delicately painted in green (page 26, below), and for the interior of Milton Abbey, Dorset, seat of the first Lord Milton, with walls rendered in a pale shade of pink.

Robert Adam has left a particularly rich legacy of colored designs, the bulk of which were acquired after his death by Sir John Soane (1753–1837) and are preserved today in the Soane Museum in London. Of all British architects, it is Adam who arguably contributed most to the development of color in painted decoration, introducing tones and combinations that were then quite new. Although popularly associated with the use of pastel colors, Adam's work was far more complex. One recent study by Ian Bristow has identified at least ten different approaches in his work simply to the allocation of color, while his palette too varied widely to encompass what he described as "Etruscan" colors, derived from antique vases, and the brighter colors employed in ancient Roman interiors, examples of which he had seen during the period he lived and studied in Italy. Not only did Adam devise the colors for interiors, he sometimes supervised the work of the housepainters who mixed them. On one occasion he was reported to have traveled all the way to Yorkshire to approve a set of color samples, the painters having busied themselves "laying on specimens of color for Mr. Adam's approbation."

Sir William Chambers (1723–96), Adam's contemporary and principal rival, also left a rich collection of colored drawings, including a beautiful green-tinted ceiling design for the London residence of the Duke of Buccleuch; another in blue for the Saloon of Pembroke House, Whitehall (page 26, top); and a wall elevation for the Great Drawing Room at Gower House, Whitehall, with a striking yet subtle combination of contrasting shades of green enlivened by pink. Contemporaries remarked on Chambers' fascination with, and mastery of, color. As the Duchess of Queensberry observed in 1772, "Sir William knows that the assemblage & blending of couleurs are Great Principals of his own masterfull supream taste." From his own correspondence, moreover, we know that Chambers might issue the most minute instructions concerning the colors his rooms should be painted. In a typical letter to Lord Charlemont in 1775 the architect informed his patron that "…the room your Lordship wants to Paint will I apprehend do best pea green in Oil with white Mouldings Cornice door & Window ornaments… Perhaps a little purple may be introduced in Some parts which if well disposed mixes well with the Green &

Opposite: John Yenn's kaleidoscopic section of a grand London mansion (above) shows this brilliant late 18th-century architect thinking not only about the color of individual rooms but of the color transitions between them and the cumulative effect they might produce together. In John Buckler's early 19th century watercolor of the Dining Room at Eaton Hall, Cheshire (below), the walls appear a brilliant "medieval" red, perfectly complementing the architecture of this remarkable Gothic Revival interior by William Porden.

White." Well aware, moreover, that color was dependent on a paint's formulation, Chambers even went as far as to specify the ingredients that painters should employ in order to produce the correct effect.

Something of Chambers' enthusiasm was evidently passed on to his pupil John Yenn (1750–1821), who produced some of the most vibrantly colored interior designs of the late 18th century, among them a dazzling section that shows the architect thinking not only about the colors of individual rooms but of the relationship between them and, indeed, the cumulative effect they might produce together (page 22, top). Edward Stevens (c. 1744–75), another pupil, also absorbed the lessons handed down by Sir William, producing another magnificent section with similarly bold transitions and juxtapositions of color worthy of the master.

James Wyatt (1746–1813) was another architect with a passion for painted decoration, and had a particular genius for matching color and form, producing interiors in which, as fellow architect Robert Smirke observed, "the Beauties of . . . Ornament and Color were so happily blended." As well as colored designs, such as that for the Drawing Room at Aldwark Hall, Yorkshire, there is the extraordinary survival of Wyatt's original painted decoration on the ceiling of the Tapestry Drawing Room at Goodwood, Sussex (page 16), which, even after two hundred years remains intact. Wyatt's contemporary, George Dance the younger (1741–1825), had an equal gift and passion for color, as is evident both from his many hand-tinted designs and from the detailed notes they contain regarding the choice and allocation of paint. Sir John Soane, who studied with Dance, also produced a large collection of annotated hand-tinted drawings, such as those of his own house in London, where an analysis of the paintwork reveals the use of stippled glazes and varnishes, reflecting an understanding that extended to the most advanced techniques and materials. Notable too at this

period was William Porden (1755–1822), whose work is represented by the brilliantly colored interiors of Eaton Hall, Cheshire, the Gothic Revival mansion he built for Lord Grosvenor, with intense reds and blues reminiscent of medieval jewelery and enamels (page 22, bottom).

Among Victorian architects, George Aitchison (1825–1910) was pre-eminent as a colorist, transposing to English interiors the colors so admired by contemporaries in the art and architecture of the Italian High Renaissance. Known as "the Artist's Architect," Aitchison worked for some of the greatest painters of his day, including Lord Leighton and George Frederic Watts, creating a range of richly decorated interiors that epitomize Victorian aesthetic taste. Another key figure of this period was the architect Edward William Godwin (1833–86) who, for clients that included Whistler and Oscar Wilde, introduced a new Japanese-inspired palette of soft blues and yellows, often executed in distemper rather than the usual oil.

The succeeding generation is represented here by one of the greatest of all English architects, Edwin Lutyens (1869–1944), a designer not generally appreciated for his use of color, but one who created schemes of sometimes startling originality. At his own house in Bloomsbury, one room was decorated with glossy black walls and an apple green floor, while at Lindisfarne Castle (pages 184–5), the interiors were painted a powerful cobalt blue and an intense forest green. Nor are the Modernists forgotten. Although philosophically and stylistically at odds with Lutyens, the Hungarian-born architect Ernö Goldfinger (1902–87) shared the latter's fascination with color, which he used to powerful effect in the house that he designed for himself in Hampstead, using contrasting planes of pure primary color to underline his uncompromising vision of modernity (pages 112–3, 194–5).

By the time Goldfinger completed work on the Hampstead house, painted decoration was passing beyond the control of architects and into the hands of interior decorators, who from the early 19th century had established themselves as an independent force in design and whose influence could be decisive. Among the early pioneers was John Crace (1754–1819), founder of a family firm that was to dominate interior decoration in England for much of the 19th century, and that first came to notice through the audacious scheme devised for the Yellow Drawing Room and other interiors at Brighton Pavilion. A particularly important figure from the 20th century was John Fowler (1906–77), of the celebrated firm Colefax and Fowler, arguably the greatest colorist of his generation, whose love affair with the 18th century found expression in the use of colors, techniques and materials freely borrowed from that time, as in the sandstone-colored decoration of the Cloisters at Wilton House, Wiltshire, (pages 98–101) and the "broken" yellow paintwork employed in the Print Room at The Vyne, Hampshire (pages 122–3). Also featured is Stéphane Boudin, head of the famous French firm of decorators Jansen, whose work at Leeds Castle in Kent for Lady Baillie in the 1930s brought the chic of interwar Paris to the chill interior of this moated Norman fortress, and at the same time introduced a whole new technique in painting to the decoration of English rooms (pages 162–3, 186–7).

Among the great decorators active in the post-war period, one who made a particularly important contribution was Felix Harbord, whose idiosyncratic, theatrical style is represented here by a previously unpublished photograph of the Venetian yellow Dining Room of the former London residence of Lord Hartwell (pages 124–5).

In the next generation, another key figure was Geoffrey Bennison, dealer as well as decorator, whose passion for *pietre dure* and the richly colored marble objects of the Baroque carried over into his use of painted decoration, producing brilliantly integrated antiquarian interiors in which colors, furniture, objects, and works of art magically coalesced.

David Hicks is arguably the most famous interior decorator of his generation, and, in terms of color, the most innovative. A true iconoclast, Hicks threw out the rule book, using colors and color combinations that staggered contemporaries and even now seem daring, powerfully evoking the heady days of the 1960s when he first rose to prominence. Hicks was adventurous both in his use of individual colors, as in the all-scarlet interior of his early 19th-century chambers at Albany, Piccadilly, and in the color transitions he created between adjoining rooms, as at Barons Court, where the visitor passes from a lipstick red staircase to a buttercup yellow dining room, a puce-colored secondary staircase, and a cream and white drawing room, with passageways painted in blue and yellow (pages 106–9, 134–7, 110–1, 66–69, 138–9). More than this, he broke with all tradition in the choice of paint type and finish, as in the decoration of his own London drawing room, where the walls were painted the color of Coca-Cola, with a top coat of high-gloss carriage varnish, while the woodwork was picked out in white with a dead matte finish.

The story of the 20th century does not end with Hicks, of course. Some of the finest examples of painted decoration are to be found in the work of contemporary decorators, most notably David Mlinaric (b. 1939), widely admired for his imaginative restorations of historic interiors, such as those at the Bath Assembly Rooms (pages 140–1, 178–9), and contemporary work, including the remarkable interior of his own house in Somerset, with its rare use of limewash (pages 196–7).

Alongside the work of architects and decorators there is the distinctive contribution made by artists. Although chiefly remembered as a painter, Dante Gabriel Rossetti (1828–82) was also a notable figure in the history of Victorian decoration, with a studio house in Chelsea that was testimony to his fascination with color. It contained a bedroom painted with Indian red walls and a forest green dado, and a parlor conceived as a meditation on the

Their glasses
in two pieces

late Georgian era, with Wedgwood blue paneling complementing a collection of Sheraton and Regency period furniture. No less arresting were the interiors devised by the illustrator Aubrey Beardsley (1872–98) for his own house in Pimlico in the 1890s. Conceived as a temple to the contemporary cult of decadence, the house contained a double drawing room with walls "distempered a violent orange," as one visitor recalled, the "doors and skirtings . . . painted black in a strange tast . . . bizarre and exotic." A few years later the painters Duncan Grant and Vanessa Bell created a magical sequence of painted interiors at their country house, Charleston, Sussex, with distemper decoration in the distinctive colors of the Omega group, of which both were leading members.

No less important is the contribution made by amateurs, some of whom stand equal to their professional counterparts. The beauty of the painted decoration in the Gallery at Castletown, County Kildare (pages 176–7) is in large part due to Lady Louisa Connolly (1743–1821), who as châtelaine of this great 18th-century Irish country house, personally involved herself in virtually every aspect of its decoration at this time. Nancy Lancaster, (1897–1994) another amateur, was especially influential. She greatly popularized the romantic faded colors found in historic houses, and the novelty of her approach can still be sensed in the decoration of the strawberry pink Entrance Hall at her country house, Kelmarsh, in Northamptonshire (pages 92–5). Mariga Guinness (1932–89) was the daughter of a German prince, but married into the famous Irish brewing family. Although she was never employed in a professional capacity, she emerged as one of the most powerful influences on interior decoration of her day and a pivotal figure in the history of color. In partnership with her husband Desmond Guinness, she revolutionized the decoration of Leixlip Castle, their Dublin base, while for friends such as Desmond FitzGerald at Glin Castle, County Limerick (pages 188–9), and the Packenhams at Tullynally in County Westmeath (pages 96–7, 192–3), she brought about a wider change in the use of paint and color, introducing the deep greens, reds and blues she remembered from the 19th-century German castles she had known as a child.

But while many of the interiors we feature are associated with famous names, some are the work of individuals whose identities are entirely unknown, anonymous designers or simple house-painters who have passed without record. We may never know who devised the striking blue paintwork in the Cook's Closet at Calke Abbey, Derbyshire (pages 180–1) or who was responsible for the deep blue decoration of the 17th-century Painted Parlor at Canons Ashby House, Northamptonshire (pages 172–5). But these and other undocumented examples are both remarkable in themselves and in the wider context of the history of painted decoration, providing a particularly poignant memorial to the tastes and practices of the period in which they were conceived. It is to the unknown men and women who created them, no less than their more famous counterparts, that this book is ultimately dedicated.

Opposite: William Chambers' design for the chimney wall of the Great Room, Gower House, Whitehall, c. 1775 (above); John Vardy's design for the south wall and alcove of the Palm Room, Spencer House, St. James's Place, 1757 (below).

PAINTS & FINISHES

LIMEWASH

Limewash is a water-and-lime-based paint with a history that stretches back over centuries. Among its many advantages, it is cheap to produce and can be mixed with a wide range of pigments. It also produces a distinctive powdery matte finish, with excellent depth of color, and ages very well. Moreover, being porous, it allows the building to "breathe," with any damp safely escaping through evaporation rather than remaining trapped within the fabric and causing possible structural problems. Limewash is especially suitable for use with limestone, lime renders and plasters, and wattle and daub.

Yet for some purposes limewash presents certain drawbacks. To the unpracticed, this apparently simple-to-use paint can give problems, resulting sometimes in fragile surfaces which may easily rub off or mark. Limewash can also be slow to dry, and causes certain pigments to darken or fade when exposed to the atmosphere. Earth pigments, such as ochres, umbers, and siennas are most commonly used with this medium. Nor is limewash suitable for use with impervious surfaces, such as hard cement renders or modern bricks, and it does not generally work well with sandstone.

Before applying limewash, the surface should be damped down with water, taking an area of approximately 3 square meters (3½ square yards) at a time, and the first coat applied thinly with a brush. When the first coat has dried out thoroughly, a process that is best left overnight, two or three further coats should be added, with light damping down between each coat. The purpose of dampening before painting is to encourage the limewash to penetrate by making the surface and substrate more permeable.

Today limewash is generally used for exterior work, but in the 16th and 17th centuries it was employed in even the grandest interiors, such as those at Hardwick Hall, Derbyshire (opposite and pages 52–3); and it may have been the example of Hardwick, as well as a preference for sober, architectural effects, that encouraged David Mlinaric to experiment with this medium in the decoration of his house in Somerset (pages 196–7). The result is a purity and simplicity that cannot be matched by any other type of paint.

Opposite: Section of limewash decoration at Hardwick Hall, Derbyshire.

LEAD PAINT

Like limewash (page 29), lead paint has a history dating back over hundreds of years, and was, until the middle of the last century, the commonly preferred choice for all high-quality housepainting in oil. Lead paint has a slightly glossy finish, resulting from the high linseed-oil content, and a "ropy," or textured surface owing to the poor flow characteristics of the lead pigment.

Lead paint was traditionally produced by grinding white lead in linseed oil, and mixing the resulting paste with additional linseed oil and oil of turpentine to thin the paint. Colored pigments could be added as required. The white lead was produced by suspending thin lead bars or coils within covered earthenware vessels filled with vinegar and then gently heating them so that the lead corroded. Already, by the 17th century, paint of this type was being manufactured and sold with the lead ready-ground and mixed with linseed oil.

Lead paint was suitable for use on virtually all surfaces, both internally and externally, and although slow to dry, it possessed the advantage that painters could go back over their work and rectify any imperfections, even after an hour or more, whereas today, with fast-drying paints, this is difficult, if not impossible. Similarly, because it was more transparent than modern paint, additional coats might be required. This naturally gave an added depth of color, and while there was a tendency for lead paints to acquire a patinated surface or "bloom," especially in darker colors, this gave a romantic "antique" appearance which to many seemed a positive attraction.

Before applying the paint, the surface would first be cleaned and repaired. In the case of woodwork, knots would be sealed using a shellac or japan size filler, while cracks would be restored using a putty containing some white lead. The surface would next be primed. Where a lighter color was to be used, a combination of white and red lead was commonly employed, producing the pink undercoat that is often found in paint analysis. Where a darker color was planned, darker primers could be used. This was then followed by at least two colored top coats. Good examples of the use of lead paint are the Painted Parlor at Canons Ashby, Northamptonshire (pages 172–5), decorated in the early 18th century, and the ceiling in the Tapestry Drawing Room at Goodwood, Sussex (pages 5, 16), which dates from the later 18th century.

Lead paint was eventually phased out and replaced by titanium, which was not only cheaper and less toxic, but also more opaque, with greater covering power, thus reducing the number of coats that were necessary. Today lead paint is used only under special licence on the restoration of the most important landmark buildings, generally on exterior rather than interior surfaces. Some conservation bodies, such as the National Trust, prefer to use safer modern alternatives for interiors, experimenting, for instance, with strengthened distempers, as at Castle Coole, County Fermanagh (pages 116–7), or with multi-layered and multi-colored glazes, to mimic the effect of early lead.

Opposite: Detail of early lead paintwork in the Painted Parlor at Canons Ashby, Northamptonshe, an interior of the early 18th century, showing the slightly shiny, "ropy" finish of this medium.

SOFT DISTEMPER

Soft distemper was used in English houses from the earliest times. The paint is made by mixing chalk with water and a little animal glue or casein, and then adding pigments. By omitting the chalk, while maintaining or increasing the level of pigment, the color of the paint can be intensified.

Soft distemper covers exceptionally well, especially on new plaster surfaces, and gives a wonderful dry, powdery finish. It is especially recommended for ornamental plasterwork, since it can be washed off and renewed, so preserving the definition of any underlying mouldings. The paint is porous, allowing the building to "breathe," and can be applied not only to new plaster but also to flat oil paint and emulsion.

One potential drawback is that soft distemper cannot be painted over in any other type of paint without the chance of causing peeling; and it also tends to be quite fragile, unlike strengthened distemper (page 34), which can withstand a greater measure of abrasion and even cleaning.

As it is relatively cheap to produce and easy to apply, soft distemper was often used in the service areas of a house, especially kitchens and larders. Here it did not matter that the paint might suffer from wear and tear and, in any case, such rooms were regularly repainted, sometimes once a year. A particularly good example, where the paint has not been renewed, is the Cook's Closet at Calke Abbey, Derbyshire (opposite and pages 180–1), untouched in over a century.

Soft distemper is no longer used on anything like the same scale as in the past; its place has largely been taken by emulsion (page 45). But emulsion can never match the subtlety and varied finish of this more traditional medium, which is best applied fairly thin, with loose, wide brushstrokes.

Opposite: Detail of the paintwork in the Cook's Closet at Calke Abbey, Derbyshire.

STRENGTHENED DISTEMPER

Strengthened distemper is the precursor of modern emulsion. It contains extra binders, such as casein and sometimes small amounts of linseed oil, and was first mass-produced in the 1870s. Like soft distemper, it has an attractive chalky finish, but does not brush off and will stand up to gentle cleaning. Strengthened distemper was used on walls where today emulsion might be employed, and in fact some formulations handle very similarly to emulsion. There are even formulations that are so well bound they can be used externally and are washable. Washable distemper, washable water paints, and paints marketed in the late 19th century as "Sanitary Paints" all fall into this category.

Best applied to plaster rather than wood, strengthened distemper covers well, and is relatively cheap to produce and easy to use. It was a particular favorite with amateur decorator Mariga Guinness, who used it on many projects, great and small, including the Library at Glin Castle, County Limerick (opposite and pages 188–9), for which she devised an intense, deep blue scheme of painted decoration for the walls.

The paint is literally saturated with color, and although some forty years have passed since the room was decorated, the blue has lost nothing of its intensity. It is noticeable that there are marked variations in the level of pigmentation, with some areas much more heavily colored than others. This can occur with distemper if the pigment is not evenly mixed and distributed. But we should not assume that the variations at Glin were an accident or the result of careless workmanship. On the contrary, Mariga deliberately created these effects to give her paintwork the appearance of age. Strengthened distemper can also be used very successfully in a thinned-down version to produce washes of color. This technique was much used by John Fowler.

A similar use of strengthened distemper is found in the Jubilee Bedroom at Tullynally, County Westmeath (pages 192–3), another house with which Mariga was associated. Here, too, the paint is unevenly applied, with marked variations in color, producing an appearance of age that is ideally suited to the 19th-century architecture of the room and the faded antique fabrics and furnishings.

Opposite: Section of the deep-blue paintwork in the Library at Glin Castle, Co. Limerick, showing the use of highly-pigmented strengthened distemper.

FLATTED LEAD

Flatted lead uses the same materials as lead paint (page 31), but the paint is rubbed down between coats and is finished with a thinned-down top coat mixed with an increased proportion of oil of turpentine, giving a smoother, matte finish. A flatted finish became fashionable around the second quarter of the 18th century, and was widely used by architects of the Palladian Revival, such as William Kent and Colen Campbell, who aimed to achieve a more sober style of decoration.

Owing to the fact that the flatting coat dried more quickly, it was necessary for painters to work together in teams, with one or two painters applying the "flatting" coat with a standard brush and another sometimes following behind with a stippling brush to smooth away the brushwork and so create an even surface. Since the final "flatting" coat tended to appear lighter than the base coat, a different shade might be used. Indeed, some early 19th-century descriptions of the use of flatted lead reveal that even the under coats and base coats varied in shade, producing a gradual accumulation of color that naturally called for visual as well as manual skill on the part of the housepainter.

The obvious difficulty and expense of applying a flattted finish meant that it was generally confined to the principal rooms of a house. This is confirmed by several early writers on painted decoration, among them John Pincot, who in his *Treatise on the Practical Part of Coach and House Painting*, published in 1811, declared that flatting was generally used only in "the best rooms, as parlors, drawing, and dining rooms." However, with modern titanium-based oil paints it is possible to achieve an in–built flatted finish by adding matting agents, without the need of a final flatting coat. The resulting formulation, generally known today as dead flat oil (page 38), is extremely popular, although inevitably there is some loss of transparency and depth of color as compared with its traditional lead–based equivalent.

Opposite: Detail of the flatted lead paintwork in the Long Gallery at Sudbury Hall, Derbyshire, as restored by John Fowler for the National Trust (see also pages 62–5).

DEAD FLAT OIL

Dead flat oil is the modern answer to traditional flatted lead (page 36), the most "noble" of all oil paints commercially available today. Produced through the use of a matte grade of titanium blended into an oil varnish, flat oil has less depth of color than its traditional equivalent, but has the advantage of an in-built matte finish that makes a flatting coat and color-adjusted undercoats unnecessary. Today it is the staple of the best interior painting in oil, having a depth of color and a matte finish that are lacking or absent in most modern emulsion paints. Dead flat oil covers in one or two coats, whereas flatted lead requires at least three, and preferably five, coats to give the same degree of cover. However, in a bid to simulate the transparency and depth of color of flatted lead, some decorators have chosen to thin down the paint and brush it on lightly or stipple it out.

Dead flat oil does not wipe clean after marking, but it can be washed quite hard; and where a wipeable alternative is called for, eggshell will sometimes provide the answer. The practice of washing down rooms rather than repainting them was often the way when there was no requirement to change the scheme. With white interiors, however, this presented obvious difficulties, making schemes of this color a particularly expensive undertaking usually confined to the houses of the very rich. John Fowler often liked to keep part of an old scheme by washing down, not only to save on expense but to preserve a link with the past. An example of this is the Long Gallery at Sudbury Hall, Derbyshire (see also pages 37 and 62–5).

Even in the restoration of the most important listed interiors, dead flat oil is generally the preferred choice. At Beningborough Hall in Yorkshire, a property of the National Trust, David Mlinaric employed modulated shades of stone and off-white in this medium to re-create the sober, architectural effect of the original 18th-century scheme, in which flatted lead would almost certainly have been used in place of the traditional lead (page 31) associated with earlier decoration.

Opposite: Detail of the Entrance Hall at Beningborough Hall, Yorkshire, showing the use of dead flat oil, a close modern equivalent of traditional flatted lead, with a sober matte finish especially well suited to architectural interiors of this kind.

GLOSS

Gloss paint is produced by omitting the matting agents normally found in oil paint and using higher levels of varnish instead. Paints of this type were produced from an early date, being used, for instance, in the decoration of carriages, but in house painting they were generally intended for external use rather than interior decoration, and although sometimes applied to woodwork, were rarely, if ever, used for walls or ceilings.

The high varnish content makes the paint flow more easily, and gives a glasslike finish with great depth of color, although it is particularly important that the underlying surface is properly rubbed down, since any unevenness will be accentuated with this medium.

The popularity of gloss increased from the late 19th century, particularly for external woodwork, especially front doors, such as the celebrated example at No. 10 Downing Street. But in interior decoration, particularly fashionable interior decoration, it continued to play little part; which is one reason why the Staircase Hall at Barons Court (opposite and pages 106–9), decorated by David Hicks in the 1970s, is so remarkable. For here, in this monumental Neo-classical interior of the early 19th century, Hicks threw out the rule book and, in a complete reversal of established practice, painted the walls in bright gloss red. As if this were not audacious enough, Hicks went further by painting the woodwork and plaster decoration matte white, so turning tradition on its head once more, while at the same time accentuating the reflective sheen of the walls. Few decorators, and fewer clients, would have had the courage even to consider such a scheme, especially in so grand and historic an interior, but Hicks and the Duke and Duchess of Abercorn, owners of Barons Court, shared the same iconoclastic, modernizing aesthetic, and together they pulled off one of the great triumphs of post-war decoration.

Nor was this a one-off. In the decoration of his own house in London, Hicks painted the walls of the drawing room in high-gloss carriage paint mixed to a color he described as "Coca-Cola;" and it is worth remembering that many years earlier, in typically quirky fashion, the architect Edwin Lutyens devised a scheme incorporating glossy black walls, apple-green floorboards and red lacquer Chinese furniture.

Opposite: In the Staircase Hall at Barons Court, County Tyrone, decorator David Hicks turned convention on its head, using gloss for the walls and dead flat oil for the woodwork and plaster decoration.

EGGSHELL

In its traditional form eggshell is an oil-based paint containing a higher than average level of varnish, giving it a slight sheen somewhere between that of flat oil and gloss, and making it both hard-wearing and easy to clean. Typically, eggshell is used on woodwork, for which, from an aesthetic point of view, it is generally considered better suited than gloss paint; and in combination with walls painted the same color but in flat oil, it produces a subtle but telling contrast, appearing slightly lighter in tone owing to its more reflective finish. Indeed, eggshell is often used where flat oil as a look would be preferred but where the paintwork requires cleaning. For this reason some eggshell paints are made flatter than others to be as close as possible to flat oil without losing the ability to be wiped clean. Water-based eggshells are freely available now as an alternative, but care must be taken to choose one that flows out well and does not leave a "ropy" or brush-marked finish.

In the late 19th and early 20th centuries, eggshell "enamel" paints were often used in kitchens and bathrooms due to their ability to be washed down, and even today the perception remains that an eggshell finish is stronger and more practical than a matte one.

In the recently redecorated 18th-century interior shown opposite, it is used as an all-over treatment for the paneling, chimneypiece and overmantel. Although the formulation is very different from that of traditional lead paint, which would have been used when the interior was first decorated, the finish is surprisingly similar, for traditional lead paint also produces a slightly reflective "oily" surface, as can be seen in the detailed photograph of the paintwork in the Painted Parlor at Canons Ashby, untouched since the early 18th century (pages 172–5).

Opposite: Detail of eggshell paintwork showing the sheen that is characteristic of this medium.

EMULSION

Early formulations of emulsion, produced from the 1950s, were essentially a new form of strengthened distemper that used artificial polymers or resins. The use of water in the paint makes it relatively cheap to produce and apply, while the polymers give durability. The concept has proved irresistible to manufacturers and consumers alike, although most modern formulations contain up to 30 percent less pigment than early emulsion formulations, and are mixed with petrochemical–based binders that produce an opaque, often shiny finish lacking in depth of color. When the level of pigmentation is maintained, and more traditional production methods are followed, the results can be quite different, and although nothing quite matches the finish of traditional oil paint, or, for that matter, distemper, some modern emulsions work extremely well, producing a softer, "flatter," and more transparent finish with greater depth of color than their mass–produced, industrial equivalents.

Opposite: Section of modern paintwork executed in a high-grade emulsion, with the soft, flat finish and strong depth of color associated with the more traditional formulations of this medium.

VARNISHED FINISH

Whereas in the 18th century a matte or flatted finish became fashionable, in the early 19th century architects and designers began to experiment with varnished finishes, which achieved the very opposite effect. This was partly an attempt to re-create the effect of the wax or "encaustic" painting associated with the decoration of ancient Roman buildings, such as those discovered at Pompeii and Herculaneum. One manufacturer of the period developed a range of "Antique Ornamental Paints," launched around 1816, which he claimed "…bear an affinity to, and answer the general purposes of, the celebrated Encaustum of the Ancients." One pioneer of this type of finish was the architect John Soane, who used a range of varnished finishes in the decoration of his own house in London. Another was Soane's contemporary and fellow architect John Nash, who, in the Picture Gallery at Attingham (opposite and pages 86–7), decorated around 1805, attempted to re-create both the finish and color of a typical Pompeian interior.

Traditionally, this type of work was produced by laying down successive coats of oil paint, each carefully rubbed down, and then successive coats of varnish, again carefully rubbed down. Color could be mixed with the varnish so as to add a particular tinge, as shown here, where the removal of the original varnished finish through cleaning has revealed a very different color underneath, a blue-black pigment having been mixed with the varnish to transform the base coat from scarlet to porphyry.

Opposite: The paintwork in the Picture Gallery at Attingham Park, Shropshire, shows the use of flatted lead overlaid with a varnish finish that is typical of the early 19th century, when this room was decorated.

STIPPLE FINISH

There are few more striking examples of the use of stippling than the painted decoration of the Duchess of Sutherland's bedroom at Dunrobin Castle in Scotland (opposite and pages 156–7). Although from a distance the colors seem to merge into one, a closer view reveals a dazzling range of different tones. The effect is produced by painting a solid base coat of color as a background and then applying a top coat in a darker color, which is dabbed and worked with a stippling brush while still wet to create the "broken" speckled finish seen here.

Stippling was especially fashionable between the two world wars, when the interior of Dunrobin was decorated, but it is rare to find examples that survive from this period, and rarer still to find examples with such highly-figured brushwork. Generally the stippling is less conspicuous, as, for instance, in the Cloisters at Wilton (page 98–101), decorated by John Fowler in the 1960s, where the stippling of the walls is combined with "dragging" to the joinery, produced, as its name suggests, by smearing the top coat to produce a streaky wash over a solid base coat.

Stippling required great skill and the involvement of two and often three different painters working simultaneously. As one painter applies the top coat, using a standard brush, the other, or others, must follow up rapidly behind and apply the stippling brush before the paint has time to dry. The technique is close to that used in applying the flatting coat to flatted lead work, although the opposite effect is produced, with brushwork stippled in rather than stippled out. Indeed, there are old descriptions of the finishing of flatted lead work that specify the use of stippling brushes for this purpose.

Normally stippling is carried out in oil, so as to allow the painters longer in which to work the paint, but some decorators, such as Fowler, preferred to work in distemper, which required particular skill and speed. It is not known who carried out the stippling at Dunrobin, but the interior is an object lesson in the use of this style of painted decoration.

Opposite: Section of the paintwork in Duchess Eileen's Bedroom at Dunrobin Castle, Scotland, a particularly good example of the highly-figured stippled finish that enjoyed such popularity at the time this interior was decorated in the 1920s.

WHITES & NEUTRALS

Whites and neutrals form a color family of exceptional breadth and diversity. White alone encompasses an almost infinite variety of different shades and tones. The history of these colors is equally rich. In fact, they have always formed the basis of English house painting. Among their many advantages, whites and neutrals are stable and relatively easy and inexpensive to produce, except for the purest whites, being based in the main on natural pigments, such as ochre and umber together with white lead and lampblack. In the period before the mid–18th century they were especially popular. Indeed they were virtually the only colors used on any significant scale. This was partly because of the technical difficulties involved in producing brighter, stronger colors, but partly also because of prevailing ideas about the sorts of colors that ought to be used in interior decoration. The traditional view was that interiors should be painted in colors approximating to those of the materials from which they were made. Whites, browns, greys, and drabs were especially popular, having obvious affinities with plaster, timber and stone, and they were generally applied to those elements composed of the corresponding material, so that ceilings were generally painted white, while paneling and joinery were often painted brown or drab. As early as the 16th century the historian William Harrison praised what he described as the "delectable whitenesse" of English plaster ceilings, while in the early 17th century the interior of Inigo Jones's Banqueting House in Whitehall was said to be painted a "white marble cullor in oyle." A few years later, at Ham House, Surrey, the paneling in the Little Hall was painted a light timber color, and in the 1690s the paneling in the Great Parlor was painted a shade of walnut.

There are numerous examples of interiors, especially entrance and staircase halls, being painted in colors approximating to stone, and in the early to mid–18th century architects of the Palladian Revival, such as Colen Campbell and William Kent, commonly used pale stones and off-whites to align their work not only with that of Palladio and of his first English disciple Inigo Jones, but with the great marble temples of ancient Rome.

Even after the introduction of brighter colors in the later 18th and early 19th centuries, whites and neutrals remained popular. Robert Adam used contrasting shades of white in the Library at Kedleston Hall (opposite and pages 56–7), and although such colors were largely displaced by the more intense shades of the Regency period, they again returned to favor in the late 19th and early 20th centuries, first through the work of second-generation Arts and Crafts designers, and afterwards by both Modernists and Classical Revivalists. In the interwar period society decorator Syrie Maugham created a design classic with her famous "all-white room" in Chelsea, a concept revived by Mary Quant in the 1960s, while in the 1970s, in a bid to break the mould of the post-war tradition established by John Fowler, David Mlinaric returned to the early Georgian palette of stones and off-whites in his redecoration of the Entrance Hall at Beningborough Hall, Yorkshire (page 72–3).

Opposite: Detail of the ceiling of the Library, Kedleston Hall, Derbyshire, first decorated by Robert Adam in the 1760s (see also pages 56–7).

HARDWICK WHITE

From the cellars to the attic, and the servants' quarters to the state apartments, Hardwick Hall in Derbyshire is painted a uniform shade of off-white. At the time the house was built, in the late 16th century, most paints were based on earth pigments and followed a muted palette, ranging from whites to stones and browns. Paint was not the dominant element but a foil to the brighter colors supplied by tapestries and fabrics, of which Hardwick possesses a particularly important collection. The type of paint employed is limewash, which, though repeatedly renewed over the centuries, conforms to the same essential formulation, based on water and lime.

The color may originally have been lighter in shade. When set against a bright white, the present color appears a deep grey, and it is possible that darkening pigments, such as yellow ochre, raw umber and lampblack, have been used over time to tone in more closely with the aging woodwork and textiles.

The use of a single color throughout the building acts as a unifying link that binds together the various interiors and strengthens the visual coherence of the whole. At the time the house was built, and in the period before the mid–18th century, the use of strong color contrasts in the painted decoration of adjoining rooms was virtually unknown.

ENTRANCE HALL STONE

It is hard to imagine a more severely architectural scheme than the black, white and stone decoration of the Entrance Hall at Osterley Park, Middlesex. Originally devised by Robert Adam in the 1760s, with plaster decoration by Joseph Rose and *grisaille* panels by Giovanni Battista Cipriani, the interior is conceived as an ancient Roman *vestibulum*. The black and grey stone floor is echoed by the walls, which are painted in two shades of grey, with the pilasters and plaster decoration off-white. The same scheme is even carried through to the furniture, which includes a set of scroll-ended stools carved with sacrificial ram masks and lion monopodia, the frames painted white and the seats covered with blue-black leather.

Paint analysis prior to redecoration was commissioned by both the Victoria & Albert Museum and the National Trust. The original scheme, in flatted lead paint, was reproduced in flat oil. All surfaces were first painted a uniform shade of stone and then picked out in the three chosen colors, using thinners to re-create the transparency and depth of color of traditional lead.

ADAM WHITE

The Library at Kedleston Hall, Derbyshire, shows the use of two tones of white. The ceiling and cornice are treated as a single entity in a paler shade than the walls below, which, by comparison, seem closer to stone or grey. Devised by Robert Adam in the 1760s, the scheme has a severity that the architect and his patron, Nathaniel Curzon, considered appropriate to a room devoted to the serious purpose of study.

The paintwork has been restored but follows both the original color and the "flatted" finish that would have been employed at this period and that was considered especially suitable to classically based interiors of this kind. Adam generally shied away from the use of strong, bright whites, and paint analysis has shown that the original color of the ceiling was a soft, muted white, achieved through the combination of earth pigments and white lead. The simplicity of the all-white scheme serves to highlight the richness and variety of the plaster decoration.

HOUSEKEEPER'S DRAB

In historic houses the best surviving paintwork is often to be found in the servants' quarters rather than the state apartments. Castle Coole in County Fermanagh is no exception. In the Housekeeper's Room there is painted decoration dating back to the 19th century, if not to the late 18th century, when the house was built. The treatment of the architectural joinery complements the natural colors of the stone columns and dry-scrubbed timber floors, including a particularly good example of Georgian "drab," as well as off-black and varying shades of white. Colors such as these were not only practical but also relatively inexpensive, deriving from the cheaper earth pigments, such as ochre and umber, as opposed to the more costly pigments used in the principal rooms above (pages 116–7). The walls and woodwork are painted in flatted lead, with the ceiling in soft distemper, and although worn and discolored, the paintwork preserves the subtlety and tonality that make this one of the finest and best-preserved interiors of its kind in the country.

An alternative and more usual approach to the decoration of such interiors was to paint all surfaces in a single color in distemper, and then to varnish those areas requiring protection, particularly the woodwork. This would produce a contrast between the lighter unvarnished surfaces and the darker varnished areas. Simple yet striking, this type of scheme was both economical and easy to renew.

LAMP ROOM GRAY

Anyone who has ever wondered about the origin of the color "Lamp Room Gray" will find their answer here. The color is taken from the walls of this lamp room at Calke Abbey, Derbyshire. Although the surface of the paint has, in the course of time, become discolored owing to the trimming of wicks and the storage of oil lamps, the underlying color can still be determined and is the basis of the popular off-white re-creation familiar today.

The type of paint is distemper, mixed to a cool grey color, most probably through the addition of "lampblack," a cheap, stable pigment that is traditionally produced by the burning of oil. Lampblack has always been the most commonly employed black pigment in house painting, but in the case of the lamp room at Calke, its use seems especially appropriate.

WASHED-DOWN WHITE

In the decoration of the Long Gallery at Sudbury Hall, Derbyshire, John Fowler showed his mastery of the art of picking out, and his remarkable ability to combine subtly differentiated shades of the same color, in this case off-white, to brilliant effect. Not that the scheme was entirely of Fowler's making. Behind a set of bookcases installed in the 19th century, sections of original paintwork had been preserved, and these were simply washed down and touched up, with only the cove and ceiling newly painted to match.

It was characteristic of Fowler to work with the grain of history. So often his interiors contain some element of an earlier scheme. Here he extends that principle to the actual preservation of historic paintwork, although the effect is not to mummify the room but rather to revive it. Decorated in the 1970s, the room takes us back to a time when the National Trust and other amenity groups took a freer approach to the restoration of historic interiors, and considered such work to be the province of the decorator rather than the paint analyst, with taste rather than science as the principal guide.

HICKS WHITE

In the Drawing Room at Barons Court, County Tyrone, decorated by David Hicks in the 1970s, we have an object lesson in the use of subtle graduated color, with several different shades of off-white combined to produce a luminous, harmonious backdrop to a rich display of works of art and furniture. The neutrality of the scheme stands in marked opposition to the flamboyant interiors elsewhere in the house (pages 106–9, 110–1, 134–9), and was clearly intended as a visual foil. The result is an interior successful both in itself and in relation to its setting, providing a tranquil interlude within a vibrant and dramatic whole.

That Hicks was able to manage and combine two such radically different approaches is a tribute to his exceptional skills as a colorist. At the same time he shows his grasp of Classical architecture, allocating color in such a way that all the various elements of the room—dado, walls, frieze, columns and ceiling—are individually expressed and at the same time collectively reconciled and balanced.

GOLDFINGER WHITE

Three shades of white are used to decorate the walls, ceiling and doors of the top-floor landing of Ernö Goldfinger's 1930s house in Hampstead. Within a Modernist framework, Goldfinger observes a traditional transition from dark to light in the relationship between the walls and ceiling, with a particularly strong reflective white for the door, that balances the brightness of the light from the circular skylight above. Here, as in the Dining Room (page 112–3) and other areas of the house, Goldfinger shows himself to have been not only a brilliant architect, but also a master of decoration, with a particular gift for using subtly differentiated colors to accentuate the architectural effects achieved through line and mass and the play of light and shadow.

OUTSIDE STONE

It was at Beningborough Hall in Yorkshire that David Mlinaric first came to full public notice as a master of architectural color and the imaginative restoration of historic interiors. Beningborough had come to the National Trust in the 1950s, and a program of restoration began in the 1970s involving John Fowler, but when ill health forced Fowler to retire, Mlinaric was appointed in his place, thus initiating a long professional association that was to encompass other major projects, such as the Bath Assembly Rooms (pages 140–1, 178–9). With a background in architectural design, Mlinaric could see at once that the Entrance Hall presented a particular opportunity. Designed in the early 18th century by local architect William Thornton, the interior represents a magisterial statement of the English Baroque. The complexity of the architectural decoration, and the uneven distribution of light, called for the most sophisticated treatment, and Mlinaric responded with a scheme that uses closely modulated shades of stone and off-white to give due emphasis to the giant Corinthian pilasters and other prominent elements within a finely-balanced overall composition.

The starting point for the scheme was the surprise discovery, through paint scrapes, that the dado in the Entrance Hall was made of stone, rather than timber. When the dado was stripped and the stone revealed, Mlinaric had the basis of his design. Several experiments were necessary before this could be achieved. Whole areas were painted, and then painted again, until the exact choice and allocation of color were determined. But in the end Mlinaric produced a scheme both internally coherent and true to the spirit of the period in which the interior was conceived. More than this, he helped establish a whole new fashion in contemporary decoration for the muted stone and drab colors of the early Georgian era.

STUDIO WHITE

The interior of this studio building in Wiltshire shows how well limewash works with timber. The off-white paint both penetrates and coats the slats and beams, bringing out the features of the wood and giving a transparency and variation in color that are the hallmarks of this medium. To help the limewash adhere, a small quantity of casein was added, and the result is a natural, hard-wearing finish whose "broken" matte appearance provides a deliberate contrast to the sheen and solid color of the bookcase, painted in oil eggshell in the color known as "studio green."

REDS

Early red paints were based on a variety of natural and manufactured pigments, of which the most common were red ochre, calcined yellow ochre, red lead and vermilion, as well as lake pigments made with dyestuffs such as carmine. There are references to the use of red in house paint from at least the early 17th century, but until the middle of the 18th century it was unusual for the color to be employed in the bright, strong form that has become familiar since. Designs by John Vardy for the interior of Milton Abbey, Dorset, in around 1755, show a pronounced shade of light red or pink for the walls, indicating the probable use of paint of this color, and similar reds also appear in a design of the same period by John Linnell, as well as a set of designs for Gopsall Hall, Leicestershire, probably of slightly earlier date. Traces of pink have been found in the alcove of the Palm Room at Spencer House in London, as indicated, once again, in designs by John Vardy of the mid–1750s.

It was around this time that traditional ideas about the use of color in painted decoration underwent a transformation, partly in response to fashions in France, with brighter, stronger colors replacing the more neutral "architectural" colors previously employed by the house painter. Reds became especially popular, with pink emerging as one of the most commonly used colors in the second half of the 18th century. Robert Adam used the color extensively, as for instance in the Eating Room at Osterley Park, Middlesex (page 154), and William Chambers also regularly employed pink in his designs, as did the architects of the succeeding generation, such as James Wyatt and George Dance.

Another dramatic shift took place in the late 18th and early 19th centuries, when the discovery and publication of the intensely colored interiors of Pompeii and Herculaneum led to the adoption of a similar palette not only in England but across the whole of Europe. It was now that the deep, dark reds of the Regency made their appearance, as in the Gallery at Attingham Park, Shropshire (pages 86–9), and other celebrated interiors, such as the Library-Dining Room at Sir John Soane's house in London and the Sculpture Gallery at Petworth, Sussex.

Powerful reds were also a feature of the Gothic Revival, with architects such as William Porden aiming to reproduce the gorgeous colors of medieval decoration, as in the scarlet Dining Room at Eaton Hall, Cheshire, also of the Regency period (page 22).

As new, more affordable pigments became available, reds were used more widely, and in the 20th century were adopted both by Modernists, such as Ernö Goldfinger, in the decoration of his own house in Hampstead (pages 112–3), and by designers in the historicist tradition, such as Nancy Lancaster, as in the Entrance Hall at Kelmarsh Hall, Northamptonshire (pages 92–5), and John Fowler, whose work includes a wide range of interiors in varying shades of red, among them the Great Hall at Ragley (pages 104–5) and the Cloisters at Wilton House, Wiltshire (pages 98–101). But for sheer nerve and brio, nothing quite matches the glossy "lipstick" red used by David Hicks in the Staircase Hall at Barons Court, County Tyrone (pages 106–9), where history and convention are brought into play only to be turned on their head, producing an interior in which the classical and the modern collide.

Opposite: Detail of the "Geranium red" paintwork in the Drawing Room at Tullynally, County Westmeath. The paint was mixed in strengthened distemper by Mariga Guinness and is typical of the intense, highly pigmented colors she employed.

PANTHEON RED

Like the architecture of the building itself, the painted decoration of the Pantheon at Stourhead in Wiltshire, looks back to Classical Antiquity. The deep red walls immediately evoke the antique vases and interiors for which the builder of the Pantheon, Henry Hoare, and others of his generation, conceived a passion. The temple dates from the mid–18th century and contains a wealth of Classical and Neo-classical statuary and reliefs. The architect was Henry Flitcroft, an associate of William Kent and Lord Burlington, but Henry Hoare involved himself in every detail. The walls are scored in imitation of stone blocking, and painted in an oil-strengthened distemper that follows the color of the original paint, from which cross-sections were taken for microscopic analysis. The plaster decoration, in off-white, matches the color of the sculpture and reliefs, variously executed in plaster, stone and lead. The iron gates are painted a deep blue, according to Georgian practice, using traditional lead paint. Completing the interior is a suite of specially designed mahogany seats of classical inspiration with carved frames and painted panels in *grisaille*.

1811 RED

The Dining Room at Dunany is like some sleeping beauty, its painted decoration virtually undisturbed for almost two hundred years. The deep red walls have never been repainted, or even retouched, since they were first decorated in the early 19th century for an ancestor of the house's present owners. Such examples are extremely scarce, and it takes little imagination to visualize the interior as it must have appeared when originally unveiled in 1811.

The color is of classical inspiration and clearly intended to evoke the ancient painted interiors discovered at Pompeii and Herculaneum in the 18th century. Similar colors are found in other interiors of the period, such as the Gallery at Attingham Park in Shropshire (pages 86–7) and the Dining Room at Sir John Soane's Museum, but the unrestored condition of the paintwork at Dunany is almost unparalleled. Nor is the surviving paintwork confined to the Dining Room. Remarkably it continues in the adjoining passageway and the Entrance Hall, where again the walls are painted "Antique" red.

The presence in some areas of a blackish "bloom" may indicate the use of vermilion in the original mix, a pigment that was particularly expensive, suggesting one reason why it was not renewed. For the seeker after pure, unadulterated examples of historic decoration touched only by the passage of time, Dunany is the stuff of dreams.

COLT HOARE RED

Red is a color found throughout the house at Stourhead. Here, in the Picture Gallery, intense red paintwork provides a particularly rich background to a collection of pictures and gems, screened in part by a curtain cunningly dyed to match.

The room was added to the house by Sir Richard Colt Hoare, who succeeded to the property on his father's death in 1787. It was Sir Richard who chose the color, which clearly reflects his love of Antiquity and his knowledge of the remains of Pompeii and Herculaneum, which he visited on his Grand Tour.

Each of the reds at Stourhead is of a slightly different shade, but it is possible that they were all originally the same color. In the 18th century a single color was often used in adjoining rooms, and even whole apartments, so as to provide a visual link between them. Although repainting has introduced variations, all the reds at Stourhead retain the same particularity of a marked blueish tinge, which may be due to the use of lampblack in the formulation of the paint or the discoloration of the main pigment, probably red lead.

PICTURE GALLERY RED

In 1805 the 2nd Lord Berwick returned from his Grand Tour with a large collection of old master paintings. The house built by his father at Attingham Park in Shropshire contained no picture gallery, nor any room that could be adapted to that purpose, so he turned to the leading architect, John Nash, to supply the want. The result was a magnificent top-lit interior of vast proportions, which remains among the grandest picture galleries ever built in England.

In the 18th century a room such as this would probably have been hung with crimson or green silk damask, as at Corsham Court in Wiltshire, or Spencer House in London. But Lord Berwick chose paint instead, although with a varnished finish, which while possibly inspired by the encaustic decoration of antiquity, may equally well have been intended to simulate the sheen of damask and velvet hangings. In some areas the original top coat of varnish has worn away, probably as a result of repeated cleaning, revealing the much brighter red of the underlying base coat. The true color can best be seen on the end walls, behind the columnar screens, where the varnish has survived and a darker, bluer red appears, close in tone to the simulated porphyry of the *scagliola* coating to the shafts of the columns and pilasters. A similar effect is produced by the painted decoration of the adjoining staircase, where the circular fluted walls literally envelop the visitor in color.

VICEROY PINK

Begun by Robert Adam but completed by his former assistant George Richardson, the Marble Hall, or "Grecian Hall" as Richardson described it, is the grandest interior at Kedleston Hall, and one of the most impressive in all of English architecture. The room was designed in 1760 for Kedleston's owner, Nathaniel Curzon, but owing no doubt to financial difficulties arising from the enormous cost of building the house, completion of the decoration was deferred until 1776–7.

The scheme was devised by Richardson, and the dusty pink color of the walls is probably based on his original designs, although repainted during the lifetime of the Indian Viceroy, the 1st Marquess of Curzon (1859–1925). Richardson worked for several years as Adam's principal draftsman, and although an important designer in his own right, his work clearly reflected the influence of his former master, particularly in regard to color. The decoration of the Marble Hall shows, how, by the 1770s color was beginning to break new ground. In earlier times entrance halls were regarded almost as part of the exterior of a house, and were painted accordingly in "architectural" colors, particularly stone. Adam himself generally followed this convention, as for instance in the Entrance Hall at Osterley Park in Middlesex (pages 54–5). But with the rise of a new generation, and a new aesthetic, designers such as Richardson broke with tradition, and in place of a steady progression from the plain to the opulent, introduced the same rich colors throughout.

LANCASTER PINK

When designer Nancy Lancaster (then married to the wealthy Anglophile American collector Ronald Tree) first arrived at Kelmarsh Hall, Northamptonshire, in the late 1920s, she found the walls of the Entrance Hall painted "a dark, rather sad green." The color was quickly swept away. Using her favorite house painter, Mr. Kick, "a true genius," as she described him, ". . . [who] instinctively understood the effect light and shade have on paint," Nancy transformed the interior through the use of a warm Italianate pink or terra-cotta color that she borrowed from Rushbrooke Hall in Suffolk, the house occupied by her friend Lady Islington. Kick was dispatched to Rushbrooke to study the paintwork there and having done so, set to work. "When it was finished," Nancy wrote, "the effect of the room was breathtaking." The artist Sir Alfred Munnings was so impressed that he immediately proposed using the room as the background to a conversation piece showing Nancy, her husband, and friends all dressed in their bright red hunting coats.

As a tenant at Kelmarsh, Nancy soon moved on, but remarkably she returned to the house after marrying its owner many years later. At that point the house was again redecorated, and it would appear that the Entrance Hall was repainted along similar lines to Nancy's original scheme. The interior has never since been touched, and the effect of the paintwork, achieved through the application of successive glazed coats of oil-bound distemper, is as striking today as it was to Nancy's contemporaries, including the young John Fowler, who used very similar colors in the decoration of various interiors of his own, including the Cloisters at Wilton House in Wiltshire (pages 98–101).

GERANIUM RED

When faced with the task of restoring the great castellated Gothic house at Tullynally in County Westmeath, Thomas Pakenham naturally turned for help to Mariga Guinness, who again showed her ability to "tame" even the grandest interiors through the use of strong, bright colors. Although she professed never to use reds in rooms with a view, here in the Drawing Room she broke that cardinal rule and, despite a truly breathtaking panorama of the surrounding countryside, employed the brightest, strongest red imaginable, dubbed "Geranium red" by the family, and as striking today as it was when originally applied over twenty years ago.

The paint itself is a distemper made by Walpamur, to which pigment has been added to the point of saturation, producing a dense matte finish and a depth of color that are Mariga's hallmark. We tend to think of such colors and finishes as traditionally Irish, which indeed they have become, although largely through Mariga's influence. It is probably truer to say that decoration of this type originates in 19th-century Europe, especially Germany, where Mariga spent a part of her formative years. Nonetheless there are some Irish precedents, including the bright orange Drawing Room at Malahide Castle and the deep blue Gallery at Castletown. It need hardly be added that at Tullynally the color in the Drawing Room does nothing to spoil the view.

CLOISTER PINK

In choosing the colors for the Cloisters at Wilton House in Wiltshire, John Fowler looked outwards to the adjoining courtyard and the rich pink sandstone of the surrounding walls. Translating what he saw into paint, Fowler used a variety of tones and techniques to achieve an effect that cleverly links the interior to the exterior, while balancing the distribution of incoming daylight. The walls are scored in a blocking pattern, simulating stone, an idea suggested by the Entrance Hall at Blithfield, Staffordshire, an interior restored by Fowler in 1953, and are painted in a rich yellow overlaid with a stippled finish of terra-cotta, using strengthened distemper. The vaulting is painted using the same materials and techniques but in a slightly paler color to compensate for the lower light levels. The ribs, door frames and skirting are all painted white with a dragged top coat of grey to simulate limestone.

As originally decorated in the early 19th century, the Cloisters were painted an even shade of greyish stone. Typically, Fowler takes an existing idea and transforms it to produce something both historically based and unmistakably modern. The interior is rightly considered one of his most successful schemes, and has been carefully conserved by the present Earl of Pembroke, whose father commissioned the work in the early 1960s.

HISTORIC RED

When asked why he had never thought to redecorate this room, the owner simply replied that the scheme was "historic." To change it would be senseless. Although one could argue with the use of the term "historic" to describe a scheme that is less than thirty years old, there is something refreshing about so conservative a view of interior decoration, which if applied more generally would have prevented the destruction of a great many first-rate interiors.

This being Ireland, the influence of Mariga Guinness is never too far distant; and, in fact, the decoration was carried out by her mother-in-law, Lady Moyne. Similar in tone to the "Geranium red" at Tullynally (pages 96–7), the color of this atmospheric Dublin dining room provides a strong but "broken" background to an idiosyncratic arrangement of Japanese prints. The color is achieved through the combination of a solid orange base coat and a deep red stippled top coat in strengthened distemper. Only on close inspection does it become clear that two different colors, and two different painting techniques, have been used to produce the one effect.

ARCHITECTURAL PINK

As originally decorated, the Great Hall at Ragley Hall would almost certainly have been painted in one or more shades of stone. It is hard to imagine the architect James Gibbs, who designed the room around the middle of the 18th century, choosing any other color for this highly architectural composition. But the 8th Marquess of Hertford, who took over the house in the 1950s, and his decorator John Fowler, opted for a thoroughly 20th-century scheme, using pink for the walls and two shades of off-white for the plaster decoration and joinery.

The scheme was not unprecedented. In the Entrance Hall at Kelmarsh Hall in Northamptonshire, another interior by Gibbs, Fowler's one time business partner, Nancy Lancaster had used a similar combination of pink and off-white (pages 92–5). But here at Ragley, it is applied on a far grander scale and in a room of yet greater importance.

It was never the intention to restore the room to its original 18th-century appearance. On the contrary, Lord Hertford and Fowler were determined to make a contemporary statement, and it was largely through color that this was achieved. Seen from an historical perspective, the scheme clearly belongs to the period immediately following the Second World War, when patrician taste shifted in favor of a light hearted, almost whimsical aesthetic as a conscious reaction against the austerity and hardship of the preceding years. But this brightly painted interior also recalls the spirit of defiant optimism with which the Hertfords, and other country-house owners of their generation, returned to their family seats following the Allied victory and, despite post-war restrictions on materials, set about restoring these buildings as the setting for a brighter future.

CARRIAGE RED

When David Hicks arrived at Barons Court, County Tyrone, in the mid-1970s, the house was painted a uniform pale green. Hicks called immediately for a bottle of port, a full set of floor plans, and three hours of uninterrupted study. By the time he finished, Barons Court had been reinvented as a kaleidoscope of brilliant contrasting colors. Nowhere is the effect more powerful than in the Staircase Hall, where Hicks had the courage to disregard all convention, choosing a deep red carriage gloss paint for the walls, strong matte white for the plasterwork and joinery, and metallic black for the balustrade. The use of gloss may perhaps have been a reference to the varnished finishes in vogue in the early 19th century, when Barons Court was built; or perhaps Hicks knew of the architect Edwin Lutyens' early experiments in this medium. Alternatively, Hicks may simply have seen an opportunity to repeat the success, on a far larger scale, of the decoration of his own London drawing room, the walls of which were painted "Coca-Cola" color using a similar high-gloss carriage paint.

Whatever his sources or intentions, the result is a scheme that reverses the usual role of gloss, normally confined to joinery alone, and so overturns the standard relationship between interior architectural elements. Improbably, the scheme provides an ideal complement to the rich Neo-classical architecture and a traditional display of 18th-century family portraits and architectural scenes by Panini. Few designers would have had the nerve, let alone the skill, to pull this off, but Hicks proved again that his fearless, iconoclastic approach to design was matched by a sure command of color and materials.

PASSAGE PUCE

In his treatment of the secondary staircase at Barons Court, David Hicks again threw out the rule book, painting the interior a deep shade of puce in modern emulsion. Hicks loved to marry the old with the new, and, piling contrast on contrast, used the modern puce paintwork as the backdrop to a traditional display of 18th-century prints in "Hogarth" frames.

Part antiquarian and part revolutionary, the scheme typifies the tensions in Hicks' work and the opposing urges that underlay so much art and design in Britain in the 1960s and 1970s.

WILLOW ROAD RED

The play of interconnecting planes of pure color make the Modernist interior of the architect Ernö Goldfinger's house in Hampstead seem almost like an early abstract painting. Rather than adopt a single color for the walls, Goldfinger used both red and white, with grey for the architrave and white for the ceiling. The scheme is a reminder of the importance of color in early Modernist decoration. It is often assumed, largely on the evidence of black and white photographs, and the work of Modernist architects today, that the early Modernists eschewed color and worked in white alone. But this is misleading.

Like other modern masters, such as Le Corbusier, Goldfinger embraced color as a key architectural tool and gave due consideration to its formulation and allocation. Here, it is deployed according to a scheme that, though based on the primary colors, avoids too simple a palette, and is organized in such a way as to emphasize the structural design of the room and the function of its various architectural components. In its own way the scheme is no less colorful, or concerned with color, than those of the pre-Modernist period. Although working in a very different idiom, Goldfinger shows himself to be the equal of any colorist among his architectural predecessors.

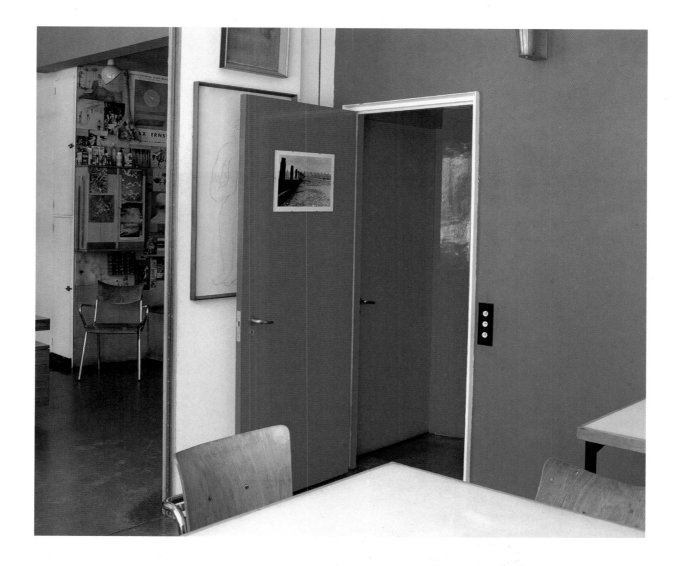

MODERN RED

Brilliant gloss red is used in conjunction with white and black in the staircase of Ernö Goldfinger's house in Hampstead to produce a scheme governed by the same stark palette as that of the French Cubist painter Fernand Léger, and the Purists, of whom Goldfinger was a particular admirer and collector. Here, as in other parts of the house, Goldfinger exploits differences in color, and differences in paint, to create a separation between the architectural elements of his design, thus emphasizing their respective functions. In this sense he uses color and paint not as decoration but virtually as architecture. While the palette ties his work to the early phase of Modernism, the allocation of color is in a tradition already well established by the 17th century, in which painted decoration served to articulate the purpose and structural makeup of a room.

OINTMENT PINK

How to produce the appearance of lead-based paint without using lead? This was the challenge at Castle Coole, County Fermanagh, when the National Trust took the decision to restore the painted decoration of this great Neo-classical house in the mid-1980s. Although lead paint would have been employed originally, its toxicity made it unsuitable for modern use, especially in a building open to the public. The solution was found in the combination of two different types of paint that together produced the required color and finish. First, a titanium-based flat oil paint was employed, of a slightly darker shade than the eventual color; and this was then overlaid with a milk-based casein paint of a lighter shade, which in conjunction with the under coat produced the desired color and a matte finish approximating to that of a flatted lead paint.

As to the color itself, this was determined through paint scrapes and cross-sections, which revealed that when the house was originally built the Staircase Hall was painted a stone color, but that in the Regency period, when the house was extensively redecorated, the interior was painted over in a pale shade of "Antique" red. This was the color re-created as part of the house's restoration, with varying shades of off-white for the architectural joinery and plaster decoration. The color was dubbed "Germolene Pink," from which came the more familiar "Ointment Pink."

YELLOWS

Yellow is today so easily produced and so widely used that it is easy to forget how difficult and limited a color it once was. For the early housepainter there was yellow ochre, a pigment that was inexpensive but relatively dull, or organic yellows, which, though bright, were fugitive and subject to discoloration. Strong, stable yellows could be produced using orpiment or lead-tin yellow, but the cost was prohibitive. It was only in the mid- to late 18th century, with the discovery of new chemical pigments, such as Patent yellow that a solution was found, although problems remained, particularly discoloration; and it was not until the introduction of chrome yellow in the early 19th century that bright, stable colors could be produced at reasonable expense.

Records do survive of the use of yellow in interior painted decoration as early as the 17th century. In the reign of James I, for instance, accounts for the decoration of the Palace of Whitehall specify the use of "yellowe" for the walls. A yellow color appears on the walls of the Portrait Gallery at Arundel House in the Strand, London, in a portrait by Daniel Mytens painted about the same period, and traces of a similar-colored paint have been discovered at the Queen's House, Greenwich, also decorated at this time.

In the 18th century the yellows grew bolder and more prevalent. A design by William Chambers for the ceiling of the Gallery at Richmond House, Whitehall, shows a strong yellow for the ground, while for Osterley Park, Middlesex, and Newby Hall, Yorkshire, the same architect devised a "limon color" for the walls of two interiors.

From the early 19th century yellow achieved even greater popularity, with chrome yellow and other newly discovered pigments allowing for deeper, stronger colors, as for instance in the Chinese Drawing Room at Brighton Pavilion, and the Drawing Room of Sir John Soane's house in London. In the later 19th century the opening up of Japan led to a vogue for oriental-style pale yellows, while in the 20th century, partly through the influence of Nancy Lancaster and John Fowler, both of whom used the color extensively, yellow entered the mainstream and is today a mainstay of contemporary painted decoration.

Opposite: Jumper Yellow. The color of the paintwork in the Dining Room at Ragley Hall, Warwickshire, was based by decorator John Fowler on a favorite bright yellow jumper belonging to Ragley's owner, the 8th Marquess of Hertford.

GONE-AWAY YELLOW

Calke Abbey, Derbyshire, is a house where time stands still, the interior virtually untouched in over a century. Nor has the house's recent restoration by the National Trust brought any real change. This is conservation rather than restoration. Nothing has been altered or disturbed, and that is as true of the paintwork as of every other aspect of the house's decoration. Crumbling, flaking and discolored, the straw-yellow distemper in the kitchen has been left in exactly the condition in which it was found. Its use reveals how, with the discovery and development of cheaper man-made pigments in the 18th and 19th centuries, bright colors of this type began to be used in all areas of large houses and not just the principal rooms.

The use of distemper was an obvious economy. In an area such as this the paintwork would have required regular renewal, and distemper, being cheaper to produce than oil paint and cheaper to apply, was the logical choice. The very fact that distemper was so regularly renewed makes its survival in this case especially remarkable.

VYNE YELLOW

In the Print Room at The Vyne, a National Trust Property in Hampshire, two great veterans, the decorator John Fowler and the architect Gerald Wellesley, joined forces to produce a gem of an interior that few would suspect dates from the 1960s rather than the 1760s. The scheme is based around a collection of engravings brought together by the National Trust's Historic Buildings Representative, Bobby St John Gore, who first conceived the idea of creating an 18th-century style print room at the house. To tone in with the engravings, which had become mottled and brown with age, Fowler and Wellesley used a related "broken" straw color, produced by means of a solid pale yellow base coat overlaid with an uneven, loosely-painted wash in a darker tone. The result is a scheme in which the walls and engravings seem to have aged together over the centuries.

Print rooms were an 18th-century fashion, but enjoyed continued popularity throughout the 19th and 20th centuries. One such interior, with a similarly variegated background, was created at Stratfield Saye, Hampshire, which Wellesley inherited on his succession as 7th Duke of Wellington in 1943.

Miracolo di S. Francesco di Paola

VENETIAN YELLOW

The interior of this 18th-century town house in Westminster is conceived as a Venetian cabinet, with glossy yellow walls simulating lacquer. The scheme was devised by Felix Harbord and dates from the late 1950s. Sometimes referred to as Felix "Cardboard," on account of his predilection for making room-models in this material, Harbord was renowned for the theatricality of his work as a designer, and the sketchy brushwork gives a consciously "stagy" appearance to the room.

Few interiors by Harbord now survive, and this is among the best preserved and most characteristic of those that do, capturing exactly the defiant mood of smart society in the post-war era and the deceptively light-hearted aesthetic that developed at that time.

JUMPER YELLOW

John Fowler surely never received a more surprising commission than the Dining Room at Ragley Hall in Warwickshire, where he was asked by the Marquess of Hertford to re-create the bright yellow color of a favorite jumper. The decoration of the room was part of a major program of works undertaken by the Marquess and his wife following their marriage in 1956. At a time when country houses were being demolished at a rate of two and even three a week, this was a brave decision, yet the revival of Ragley turned out to be one of the great achievements of post-war patronage in England, demonstrating that country houses still had their part to play in contemporary design.

Typically, Fowler used a variety of materials and techniques to achieve the one deceptively simple effect. First he applied a solid base coat of pale yellow in flat oil, and then, using a thinner, darker solution as a glaze, he added a finishing coat to produce a "broken" surface in which the two different paints and colors combine as one.

SUDBURY YELLOW

By the time Sudbury Hall in Derbyshire came to the National Trust, this great 17th-century house had largely been shorn of its contents and stood virtually empty. Through the use of color, John Fowler restored the house to life. Using virtually no other materials besides paint, he managed to conjure up the atmosphere of a functioning family house.

The scheme devised for the Staircase Hall owed little to history, and even at the time caused controversy. Although a precedent existed for the white-painted woodwork, the yellow of the walls was utterly new. Indeed, a bright yellow such as this would have been all but impossible to achieve when the interior was first created in the late 17th century; and the use of distemper might be considered inappropriate in a grand interior that would almost certainly have been painted in oil. But no one can deny the energy and confidence of this late 20th-century intervention, while the uneven color and conspicuous brushwork cleverly simulate both age and the "ropy" effect of early lead-based paintwork. Now the debate is whether the scheme should ever be replaced. Thirty years on, Fowler's work has acquired its own historical importance and legitimacy, and, ironically, the only controversy today is whether it ought not to be preserved.

BUCKRAM YELLOW

The Dining Room at Barons Court, Co. Tyrone, demonstrates the influence that surface has on color. Commissioned to redecorate the interior in the 1970s, David Hicks chose not only to repaint the walls, but to line them, choosing a rough bookbinder's buckram, which he then painted a warm shade of yellow in strengthened distemper. The same paint applied to a different surface would not have produced the same color. The rough, uneven texture of the buckram also provides a contrast to the smooth precision of the plasterwork and the carved decoration of the ornamental joinery, a typically subversive touch.

Historically, the scheme is brazenly at odds with the architecture, which another decorator might have painted in the tones of the early 19th century, when the room was designed. But Hicks imposed a typically defiant, unapologetically modern solution, rather than take the historicist approach, using the tension between the old and the new to inject drama and energy into this towering Neo-classical rotunda.

PASSAGE YELLOW

In the passageway at Barons Court, David Hicks again shows his love of strong, bright colors, and his interest in color contrasts and transitions. An intense, rich yellow at one end gives way to deep, dark blue at the other, with the terra-cotta paintwork of the Entrance Hall glimpsed beyond. Here, as so often in his work, Hicks issues a series of visual jolts to create excitement and drama. As a designer, he thought not only about the treatment of individual rooms but of the relationship between them and of the cumulative effect they produced together.

At Barons Court each interior has its own distinctive character, but it also has a part to play within its immediate setting and the house as a whole. In this respect the passageway is no less important than the great set pieces, such as the Staircase Hall and the Dining Room (pages 106–9, 134–7), and its treatment reflects the same high level of attention. Beyond the use of paint, Hicks also varies the level of the dado or skirting between rooms, and at the same time uses works of art and painted and gilt furniture to introduce their own sharp bursts of contrasting color.

Although some thirty years have passed since it was originally decorated, the interior remains in pristine condition, a tribute both to Hicks' lasting appeal and the outstanding care with which the owners of Barons Court have preserved this single most important surviving example of his work.

OCTAGON YELLOW

Over the years David Mlinaric has mixed literally hundreds of original colors for historic and contemporary interiors. Here, in the Bath Assembly Rooms, a building of the mid-18th century, he devised a muted yellow as a prelude to the blue of the adjoining Ball Room (pages 178–9). The understatement is typical of Mlinaric's work as a colorist, and the dead flat finish true to the period of the building.

Unlike John Fowler and David Hicks, with whose work his own briefly overlapped, Mlinaric uses color in a subordinate role to architecture. In a Mlinaric interior color quietly takes its place in support of a scheme that begins and ends with the architectural design. The harmony is such that the colors, however strong, appear subdued, and however newly painted, intrinsic to the room.

CONNECTING YELLOW

Purity and a respect for natural materials are the principles governing the decoration of this passageway, conceived by David Mlinaric in the 1990s. Luminous yellow limewash brings out the natural texture of the plain plaster walls, with the timber floor left plain and unvarnished. Through a door at the far end we can glimpse another interior, also painted in limewash and similar in tone, although in blue, providing a striking though subtle contrast.

As a former architecture student who has spent a lifetime studying historic buildings, Mlinaric instinctively understands the concept of hierarchy and progression, and the need to match decoration to the status and function of a room. Here he responds to, and even emphasizes, the simplicity of the setting, deliberately using a type of paint traditionally associated with vernacular decoration. It is one of Mlinaric's greatest gifts as a decorator that he is able to make color appear integral to a room, as if it had developed naturally from the architecture. In this case the use of limewash strengthens this impression, since the paint, having penetrated and fused with the walls, not only seems to form part of the architecture but is literally inseparable from it.

GREENS

In one of the earliest recorded references to painted decoration in England, Henry III ordered the panelling of his principle residence to be painted green. The exact color of this 13th-century scheme is unknown, and may have been relatively subdued; for the only bright pigments available to the house painter at that time, and, indeed, before the 18th century, were ruinously expensive, even by royal standards, or else unstable or incompatible with simple house paint. Where bright greens were employed, they were generally confined to decorative details rather than the larger surfaces of walls and ceilings, and most interiors were painted in the muted greens and olives familiar from the backgrounds of early Georgian portraits. These are the colors we should bear in mind when reading the accounts of 17th-century house painters, such as those relating to the decoration of the Lord Steward's apartment at Whitehall in the 1620s or of Henrietta Maria's rooms at Wimbledon House in the 1640s. Perhaps, too, it was to colors in this range that the architect and painter Balthazar Gerbier referred in his *Counsel and Advise to All Builders*, published in 1663, when he recommended the use of "fairest green" for panelling; and similar colors may also have been employed when, in the 1690s, areas of the royal palaces at Whitehall, Kensington and Hampton Court were redecorated in green for William III.

Despite the introduction of Prussian blue in the early 18th century, which made it easier to produce brighter greens, olives and drabs remained the fashion for many years, and in the mid-1750s the architect John Vardy was still working within this palette in his designs for Spencer House in London. It was only in the next generation, through the work of Robert Adam and William Chambers, that bright greens began to be used more widely. At his own house in London, Chambers used such colors, also recommending them to clients, both for plasterwork and joinery. Closely related colors were likewise used by Adam, as for instance at Harewood House in Yorkshire, and at Osterley Park in Middlesex (pages 146–9, 154–5), and in the succeeding generation James Wyatt and George Dance followed in the same direction. By this time new pigments were becoming available, including Brunswick green and Scheele's green, both inventions of the second half of the 18th century, and further discoveries in the 19th and 20th centuries gave added impetus to the trend towards stronger, brighter colors in this range. In the mid-19th century the Pre-Raphaelite painter Dante Gabriel Rossetti had his bedroom in London painted a strong forest green, and another strong Victorian green is found in the Breakfast Room at Calke Abbey, Derbyshire (pages 152–3). Sage greens enjoyed a particular fashion during the Arts and Crafts period, while Celadon green became the rage between the wars, inspired by the parallel vogue for oriental ceramics, as in the decoration by Stéphane Boudin of the Dining Room at Leeds Castle in Kent (pages 162–3). In the Drawing Room at Biddesden, Wiltshire (pages 164–5), another interwar interior, we seem to return to the 18th century, with bright green made brighter still through the juxtaposition of a sharply contrasting shade of pink.

Opposite: Pea Green. The paintwork in the Gallery at Osterley Park, Middlesex is a modern re-creation of a scheme of the 1760s described in a contemporary account as "pea green." The exact shade was taken from a surviving piece of original 18th-century fabric backing to the seat furniture.

PALMER GREEN

Paint analysis has allowed for a near-exact reconstruction of Robert Adam's original 1770s scheme of decoration in the Staircase Hall at Osterley Park, Middlesex. Under the direction of Anthea Palmer, Historic Buildings Representative at Osterley, two shades of green were employed for the skirting and walls, the former being darker than the latter, as was traditional, with off-white marking out the ornamental joinery and plasterwork. In accordance with Georgian practice, the wrought-iron balustrade was painted blue rather than black, as is also the case in the Pantheon at Stourhead (page 80).

The green of the walls provides an obvious visual link to the color of the walls in the Gallery (pages 148–9), where the decorative scheme may also have been devised by Adam. The restoration was achieved using two different tones of green and two different types or consistencies of paint. Although barely visible, except on close inspection, a solid base coat was first laid down in flat oil, over which a wash of thinned flat oil was applied to give the paintwork added life and depth of color.

PEA GREEN

The Gallery at Osterley Park, Middlesex, is something of a puzzle. The chimney piece is close in design to the work of William Chambers, although there is no evidence that Chambers worked on this room, whereas the frieze is of a style associated with the Palladian Revival, although again it is not known which Palladian architect might have been responsible. The structure of the room, 40 meters (130 feet) in length, is older still, yet its origins are hard to fix. Nor can we be sure who devised the scheme of painted decoration, for there is no certain proof. The likelihood is that Robert Adam was involved, for he carried out extensive work at Osterley from the 1760s for the house's then owner, the banker Robert Child, and the choice and allocation of colors are paralleled in other examples of his work. Moreover, he is known to have made structural alterations to the Gallery, while the green of the walls closely relates to that in the Staircase Hall (pages 146–7), for which Adam was certainly responsible. Typical, too, is the combination of green with pink, which is used in the decoration of the dado and the frieze. A similar combination is found in the Eating Room at Osterley (pages 154–5), again perhaps by Adam.

A contemporary description of the Gallery at Osterley specifies that the walls were hung with a paper stained "pea green." Although the paper itself had long disappeared when the room came to be restored in the 1980s, a similar, if not identical, color was found on the fabric lining the backs of the seat furniture, and this was simply replicated in paint.

MITCHELL GREEN

The strong green paintwork in the Picture Gallery at Stourhead, Wiltshire, is a reconstruction of the original scheme, based on microscopic analysis and executed in the 1990s for the National Trust. The work was conceived by Anthony Mitchell, Historic Buildings Representative for Wessex, and entrusted to the firm of Hesp and Jones, successors to a painting company often used by John Fowler. To produce the right shade of green, while simulating the effect of traditional flatted lead, the painters used two different colors for the base and top coats, the former a slightly yellower green, the latter more blue. Together with crimson, green was considered the most appropriate background to paintings in the 18th and early 19th centuries, and its use here is typical of the period. The dead flat finish accentuates the brilliance of the giltwood frames, also giving a gemlike appearance to the paintings.

CALKE GREEN

The Breakfast Room at Calke Abbey, Derbyshire, retains a scheme of painted decoration that is virtually untouched since the Victorian period. Especially striking are the walls, painted a strong shade of green and edged with a simple giltwood fillet. The paintwork sheds light not only on the color preferences of the Victorian period but also on the materials and techniques employed by painters at this time. As one would expect in a room of this importance, a traditional lead-based oil paint has been used, applied in successive coats—possibly as many as five—with a finishing coat of a slightly different tone, giving remarkable depth of color and a lively, varied surface. The use of lead paint is virtually prohibited today, owing to its toxicity, which makes it difficult for the modern painter to reproduce such effects from the past. But the Breakfast Room at Calke, as a particularly well-preserved example of this type of paintwork, provides an excellent guide to those attempting to re-create such effects by other means. A detail can be seen on the cover and contents pages.

FEASTING GREEN

A bright Neo-classical green, originally painted in the 1760s and renewed in the 19th century, fills the background to the white plaster decoration of the wall panels in the Eating Room at Osterley Park, Middlesex, decorated for the banker Robert Child by Robert Adam. Broad borders of pink bring contrast and added intensity, recalling the similar effect achieved by John Vardy in the decoration of the coffering in the alcove of the Palm Room at Spencer House. The combination of pink and green is often found in interiors of this period, reflecting the wider fashion for brighter colors and color contrasts that resulted in part from technical breakthroughs in the manufacture of suitable pigments in the first half of the 18th century.

Adam was especially renowned for his use of pale "pastel" colors, and the Eating Room at Osterley is typical of this approach, which was widely imitated by Adam's contemporaries and continues to be practiced today, with decorators commonly referring to "Adam" colors. However, it is worth remembering that Adam worked in a variety of different palettes, sometimes using stronger, darker colors than those seen here, as well as the neutral, muted tones exemplified by the Library at Kedleston Hall, Derbyshire (pages 56–7). Moreover, as an architect concerned as much with the function of a room as with its decoration, Adam used color expressively, and in the Eating Room at Osterley, an interior conceived as a temple to feasting, he uses bright, spirited colors to strike an appropriately festive note.

STIPPLE GREEN

Dunrobin Castle, a Loire Valley château set down on the north-east coast of Scotland, has a complex building history and a history of ownership to match. Built on the site of an earlier house by Sir Charles Barry, architect with A. W. Pugin of the Houses of Parliament, Dunrobin was badly damaged by fire in the early 20th century and afterwards rebuilt by Sir Robert Lorimer, sometimes referred to as "the Scottish Lutyens." The original owners were the Dukes of Sutherland, but the house was occupied for a time by a school and today belongs to the Countess of Sutherland, to whom it passed on the death of her uncle, the 5th Duke, in 1963.

Right at the the top of the house is a chic 1920s apartment created for Duchess Eileen, the beautiful and flamboyant wife of the 5th Duke. The Duchess's bedroom, designed in a style combining elements from the Louis XVI and Directoire periods, is paneled with *boiseries* painted a vibrant shade of green, with gilt enrichments. The technique used in the painting of these *boiseries* reflects the interwar fashion for "fancy" finishes. In this case a solid basecoat of pale green oil paint was applied and then overlaid with a darker glaze, using a coarse stippling brush to produce a particularly highly-figured finish that flaunts rather than masks its artificiality. A detail can be seen on page 49.

LUTYENS GREEN

The deep forest green paintwork at Lindisfarne Castle, on Holy Island, is a reminder that Sir Edwin Lutyens, who devised the scheme for Edward Hudson, owner of *Country Life*, during the Edwardian period, was not only an outstanding architect but also a brilliant and audacious colorist who used splashes of dense, highly pigmented paint to animate the interior of this ancient island fortress. The green makes an interesting comparison with the intense cobalt blue decoration used elsewhere at Lindisfarne by Lutyens (pages 184–5) and reveals a side to the architect that has generally been disregarded.

Like his 18th-century predecessors William Kent and Robert Adam, Lutyens was concerned not only with the structural design and architectural decoration of the houses on which he worked, but with their every detail, especially the choice and allocation of paint. Here he shows himself to be flamboyantly at odds with the reputation he has today as a designer little interested in decoration and a tame follower in the Arts and Crafts tradition of muted, neutral colors. There could, in fact, be no greater contrast between his own work at Lindisfarne and the sage greens and pale blues and yellows espoused by his immediate predecessors.

CELADON GREEN

A celadon green was chosen by Parisian decorator Stéphane Boudin as the dominant color in the Dining Room at Leeds Castle in Kent, providing a suitably delicate accompaniment to the muted tones of the 18th-century tapestries, painted furniture and *famille rose* china. Using a technique pioneered in France, and one he often used as a decorator, Boudin applied a solid base coat of pale green flat oil paint to the paneling, mixed to a slightly lighter tone than the eventual color, and then used a wax bar, dabbed in pure green pigment of a darker tone, to coat the surface with a soft, variegated finish.

The scheme dates from the mid-1930s when Boudin, then at his peak, was summoned to England by Lady Baillie, the owner of Leeds Castle, who had purchased the property a few years earlier. Lady Baillie was the epitome of the Anglo-American patrician. Her mother was a member of the wealthy Whitney family, US patrons of the arts, and her father an English Lord. She had also spent a part of her childhood in France and could converse with Boudin in perfect French. The two clearly got along. In addition to the Dining Room, Boudin also devised the decoration of Lady Baillie's private apartment (pages 186–7) and eventually took sole charge of the whole interior.

Leeds is one of several English castles restored between the wars, but Boudin's contribution makes the building unique, bringing a flavor of interwar Parisian chic to the interior of this battlemented Norman fortress.

30s GREEN

Combinations of green and pink are often found in 18th-century interiors, such as the Eating Room at Osterley Park (pages 154–5). But here in the Drawing Room at Biddesden in Wiltshire, the brightness of the colors and their powerful contrasting relationship mark this out as an obviously 20th-century interior. The scheme dates from the 1930s, and was devised by the fashionable London decorator and antique dealer Dolly Mann, although the building itself was originally erected in the early years of the 18th century for one of the Duke of Marlborough's generals.

No picking out is used, so that nothing diminishes the impact when the two plain colors collide; and the same clash of pink and green is carried through to the relationship between the paneling and the window curtains and lampshades. The paint itself is a dead flat oil.

Like all the interiors at Biddesden, the Dining Room reflects the interwar revival of interest in 18th-century decoration, and a knowledge of its principles and practices, while at the same time embracing the creative opportunities of the modern age.

LUNCH GREEN

The Dining Room at Biddesden in Wiltshire, created out of two early 18th-century interiors, is loosely painted in a thin, flat oil paint to create a translucent matte finish that naturally brings out the texture and character of the underlying paneling. No attempt is made at picking out, and there is none of the fussiness and over-elaboration that so many decorators mistakenly believe is called for in historic rooms.

The scheme reveals how altering the consistency of paint and the technique used to apply it can transform the resulting color and finish. A muted green is perfectly complemented by the transparency of the paint and light brushwork. The scheme is assertive yet restrained, and takes its proper place as the background foil to the room's fine architectural detailing and a display of early 20th-century British art.

GREEN STONE

The creation of color harmonies between the diverse elements of an interior is one of the features of 18th- and early 19th-century decoration. Here, in the Staircase Hall at Stourhead, restored in the 1990s, the walls have been painted a pale stone green to match the color of the marble inlay at the center and along the borders of the floor. The joinery and plasterwork similarly tone in with the main area of the floor, creating an interplay of closely related whites. The original lead-based oil paint has been renewed using a modern flat oil paint, specially mixed and applied to achieve a similar finish and depth of color.

BLUES

Until the discovery of Prussian blue, a strong, bright pigment that was both economical and stable, and that was first developed by a Berlin color-maker in the early 18th century, the use of blue in house painting was extremely limited, being restricted in the main to details and generally available only to the very wealthy.

Blue could be achieved using indigo, a plant dye, but the color this produced was relatively dull, with a tendency to fade. The only real alternatives were smalt, a form of crushed blue glass; azurite, a naturally occurring mineral; blue verditer, its artificial equivalent; or ultramarine, produced from lapis lazuli. However, the cost of these pigments, especially ultramarine, was considered by most to be excessive, and there were difficulties also in using them in simple house paint. For this reason there are few known examples of English interiors incorporating blue painted decoration on any scale before the 18th century.

In the 16th century an azurite-based paint was used in the interior known as Wolsey's Closet at Hampton Court, but this was confined to the ground of the ceiling. In the 1620s and 1630s a similar paint was employed at the Palace of Whitehall, but again in small quantities as a means of picking out. At the same period, in the Queen's Cabinet at the Queen's House, Greenwich, a smalt-based paint was used, although only on sections of the ceiling and entablature, and in the 1690s the King's Painter, Robert Streeter, used a "fine smalte" on the famous "Tulip Stairs," but only on the ironwork of the balustrade. Similarly, a paint based on blue verditer was employed at Whitehall in the 1620s, but, again, only selectively on a limited number of elements.

All this changed with the introduction of Prussian blue, which for the first time made blue a color that could be used by the house painter on larger areas and for a wider clientele. In 1748 the Earl of Chesterfield ordered the French-style Boudoir at Chesterfield House, London, to be painted all over in a "beau bleu;" and strong blue paints were also employed or recommended by William Chambers for the decoration of Pembroke House and Gower House in Whitehall, as well as the Casino at Marino, near Dublin, in the 1760s and 1770s.

The development in the 19th century of other pigments, notably artificial ultramarine, had a similar liberating effect, and from this time forward the color enjoyed enormous popularity.

Opposite: Irish Georgian Blue. The paintwork in the Gallery at Castletown, County Kildare, closely follows the color of an original Neo-classical tablet in the center of the chimney piece. Originally designed for the Connolly family in the mid-18th century, the interior was restored some two hundred years later by Desmond and Mariga Guinness, leading figures in the Irish Georgian Society.

PARLOR BLUE

The Painted Parlor at Canons Ashby in Northamptonshire typifies the dark Baroque palette of late 17th- and early 18th-century painted decoration. The interior was created during the occupation of Edward Dryden (d. 1717), a cousin of the famous poet, and was almost certainly conceived and executed by another family member, Mrs Elizabeth Creed (1642–1728), possibly assisted by her daughter, Elizabeth Steward. Both were talented amateur artists and designers, and are known to have worked on similar schemes elsewhere.

The combination of dark blue and timber-brown is especially striking, and illustrates the point that before the development of bright pigments for house paint in the early to mid-18th century, most of the colors employed by house painters in England were relatively muted. At the same time, the surface shows the slightly shiny, "ropy" finish of early lead-based paint, as distinct from the smoother, matte flatted finish that became fashionable from the middle of the 18th century.

The Painted Parlor retains the atmosphere of an interior virtually untouched by time. Three hundred years of changing fashion have passed almost without effect. Few rooms have as much to teach us about historic paint and color.

IRISH GEORGIAN BLUE

The restoration of the Gallery at Castletown, County Kildare, is one of the crowning achievements of the Irish Georgian Society, and of Desmond and Mariga Guinness, the couple who did so much to revive its fortunes. It was Desmond Guinness who purchased Castletown when the great 18th-century house was sold in 1967 and then gave it to the Society; and it was Mariga who, with Desmond, masterminded the restoration of the interiors, which are among the most magnificent of their date in Ireland.

The blue of the Gallery walls, which follows the color of the Neo-classical plaque in the center of the chimneypiece, is a 19th-century repainting of an original mid-18th-century scheme and typifies the cool but strong palette of that period, powerfully evoking the glory days of Castletown, when the Gallery was the setting for lavish receptions hosted by Tom "Squire" Connolly and his English-born wife, Louisa, a daughter of the Duke of Richmond. It was Louisa no doubt who oversaw the decoration of the room, which was carried out by a painter who had earlier worked at Goodwood, her family house in Sussex. Louisa's passion for interiors is evident throughout the house, and it is clear she had a particular love and understanding of color.

With the arrival of Desmond and Mariga Guinness some two hundred years later, it was as if history were repeating itself, and the Gallery stands as a monument to their work and the revival they fostered in the appreciation of the fine and decorative arts of 18th-century Ireland.

BALL ROOM BLUE

Cavernous in its structure yet minute in its detailing, the Ball Room at the Bath Assembly Rooms presents an obvious challenge for any decorator in terms of the choice and allocation of color. When the interior was restored in the late 1970s the National Trust turned to David Mlinaric, whose early training at the Bartlett School of Architecture had given him a particular knowledge and understanding of Classical architecture.

Taking his cue from an earlier scheme, Mlinaric chose a dusty pale blue, offset by stone, producing an impression that is festive yet stately, as befits a magnificent 18th-century interior originally intended as a setting for sumptuous public receptions. The balancing of the tones between the blue and stone, and the picking out of details such as the frieze, show a particular mastery of color and its relationship to architecture.

COOK'S BLUE

Untouched in over a century, the bright blue paintwork in the Cook's Closet at Calke Abbey, Derbyshire, has lost none of its intensity, although clearly showing the effects of time. Here, as in the kitchen (pages 120–1), the paint is a soft distemper, a water-and-chalk-based paint which produces subtle variations in color and a powdery, milky finish. Blue is often found in historic houses in areas where food was stored and prepared, one explanation being that the color was thought to be repellent to flies.

Under normal circumstances the paintwork would have been regularly refreshed, possibly once a year, but the owners of Calke ceased making repairs or alterations quite early in the house's history, so that the Cook's Closet, along with other interiors, has come down to us as a virtual time-capsule from the 19th century.

The name of the painter responsible for the decoration is unrecorded, and he probably saw nothing remarkable about his work here. Probably he would be shocked by the condition of the paintwork and amazed that it had not long ago been renewed. But to modern eyes the painter's choice of color seems extraordinary, and the condition both poignant and romantic.

CHIRK BLUE

Chirk Castle in Wales dates originally from the 14th century, with magnificent Neo-classical plaster decoration of the 1770s, but the brilliant blue paintwork seen here belongs to the 1840s, and was conceived by the partnership of architect A. W. Pugin and decorator J. G. Crace, best known for their work on the Houses of Parliament. A love of rich, deep colors was typical of the period, but even by contemporary standards this was exceptional. A party of visitors in the 1850s was shocked by the ceiling's "bright blue," and Crace himself was forced to defend the scheme in the pages of *The Builder*.

The combination of blue and gold is found in English decoration from at least the mid 16th century, but few examples achieve the same saturated intensity as the ceiling at Chirk, which looks back beyond the early 17th century to the gorgeous colors of the Middle Ages and the Renaissance, and so to the period when the castle was built. The paint is oil rather than distemper, but having never been renewed, the underlying plaster decoration is still extremely crisp, while the color remains strong, so that it is possible to enjoy the work of Crace and and Pugin more or less as it would have appeared to contemporaries.

LUTYENS BLUE

As a colorist, Lutyens is generally associated with the pale, neutral tones of the later phase of the Arts and Crafts style and the Queen Anne and Baroque Revival. But as his work at Lindisfarne Castle reveals, he was not afraid to use bright, strong colors when the opportunity presented itself.

Lindisfarne, the ancient island fortress, was remodeled by Lutyens as an occasional retreat for its then owner Edward Hudson, proprietor of *Country Life*. In the Dining Room, the architect coated one whole wall of the solid stone interior with a deep cobalt blue paint so densely colored that it seems to consist of nothing but pigment.

Lutyens has been studied almost exclusively in his role as architect, but the interior at Lindisfarne makes clear that he was intensely interested in decoration, and more particularly painted decoration, and that his approach to color was no less inventive and idiosyncratic than to architectural design.

BOUDIN BLUE

In the design of Lady Baillie's Bedroom at Leeds Castle in Kent, Parisian decorator Stéphane Boudin succeeded in creating the illusion of a French interior of the 18th century. It is partly the *boiseries* and the Louis XV chimneypiece with its *trumeau de glace* and inset flower painting, but central to the overall effect is the painted decoration, which constitutes a rare example of a peculiarly French technique in England. After first rubbing down the wooden panelling with a wire brush to bring up the grain and create an "aged" surface, Boudin's team of painters applied a solid coat of off-white, followed by a "dragged" coat of blue. This was then sealed using a bar of wax dabbed in pure pigment, and finally the surface was lightly distressed to reveal tiny specks of white in the underlying base coat.

A similar scheme was devised by Boudin for the Dining Room of the Duke and Duchess of Windsor's house in Paris after the Second World War, but the bedroom at Leeds Castle is earlier, dating from the 1930s, and, among surviving English interiors of that period, probably unique.

English interiors have always reflected continental influences, the result not only of foreign travel and trade, but of the presence in England of patrons, designers and artist-craftsmen from abroad. Boudin's work for Lady Baillie can be seen in a tradition that dates back centuries, yet the bedroom and other interiors at Leeds Castle belong to a particularly cosmopolitan period in English decoration, when England became, for a time, a social and economic magnet for smart society the world over. Originally built by Norman conquerors, Leeds Castle was perhaps the ideal setting for this remarkable later flowering of England's cross-cultural tradition in design.

KNIGHT'S BLUE

The Library at Glin Castle, County Limerick, is among the earliest and best-preserved examples of the work of Mariga Guinness, featuring a bold scheme of dark blue and strong white that is typical of this brilliant and original designer. Undertaken in the late 1960s for friend and fellow "Irish Georgian" Desmond FitzGerald, the Knight of Glin, the interior has affinities with the strong blue decoration of the Dining Room at Bantry House, County Cork, and the Chinese Room at Carton, County Kildare; but nothing quite matches the depth and intensity of the blue at Glin, which, like other of Mariga's colors, ultimately looks back to the 19th-century German palaces in which, as a member of the royal house of Württemberg, she spent a part of her youth.

Colors of this type have since been absorbed into the Irish mainstream; today we regard them as typically and traditionally Irish. But this is merely a mark of Mariga's influence. The Library at Glin is a reminder that these colors were in fact introduced from abroad, by a foreigner working in the latter part of the 20th century. As ever with Mariga, the paint is a strengthened distemper, pigmented to the point of saturation and mixed by hand so as to produce an uneven distribution of color that brings both variety and a strong human quality to the finished work.

BIDDESDEN BLUE

High up in the attics at Biddesden in Wiltshire is this bright blue interior with paintwork dating from the 1930s. The color has lost nothing of its original intensity or its power of surprise, and is more Portuguese *quinta* than English country house. Nothing could be further removed from the muted colors in which this early 18th-century passageway would originally have been painted. The elaborate picking out in contrasting shades of white is another typically 20th century touch.

JUBILEE BLUE

Taking her cue from the soft blue-green colors of the surrounding landscape, Valerie Pakenham devised a suitably restful scheme of decoration for the Jubilee Bedroom at Tullynally, County Westmeath, seat of the Pakenhams, Earls of Longford, since the mid–17th century. The room is painted in a distemper known as "Jubilee Blue," produced by the well-known manufacturers Walpamur. The paint is freely and unevenly applied, with animated brushwork left visible to produce a painterly, translucent finish as soft and subtle as the color itself. All memory has been dispelled of the previous scheme, a solid pale custard color dating from before the War. Instead we have a scheme that, though conceived in the mid–1960s, seems closer in spirit to the early 19th century, when this interior was originally built and decorated.

The use of distemper, and the uneven finish, immediately suggest the influence of Mariga Guinness, a close friend of the Pakenhams, who advised on the decoration of Tullynally, and is thought to have mixed the color for the Geranium Drawing Room (pages 96–7). Mariga often worked with distemper in this way, deliberately introducing variations in pigmentation and brushwork to simulate the effect of historic paints and techniques, and the passage of time. The result, as here, was a style of painted decoration that brilliantly evoked the past while providing the perfect complement to the antique furnishings and other historic contents of a room.

GOLDFINGER BLUE

Built for his own occupation by the émigré Hungarian architect Ernö Goldfinger, the house at 2 Willow Road in Hampstead reveals an approach to design that is far removed from the stereotype of Modernism. The interior is painted not in white alone, nor solely in the primary colors, but in muted, intermediate colors ranging from a deep terra-cotta red to battleship grey, and here, in the architect's own office, white and pale blue.

Goldfinger was a committed Modernist and a particular admirer of the Purists, whose approach to color was highly prescriptive, but his own approach to color, like that of his contemporary Le Corbusier, was surprisingly sensual and imaginative, providing a counterbalance to the austere abstraction of his architecture. This is not to say that Goldfinger, still less Le Corbusier, used color only in a decorative way. Throughout the house, but very obviously here in the office, paint is applied in solid, clearly demarcated planes, with only minimal picking out to the joinery. This creates a lively interplay of contrasting colors, but also underscores the subdivision of the interior into its constituent architectural elements: color in the service of function.

The paint itself is a typical early emulsion, that is to say a water-based paint, or distemper, strengthened with oil, although with fewer of the petrochemical or plastic binders that give most modern-day emulsions a hard, slightly reflective finish.

MONSTER BLUE

There is nothing arbitrary about the colors chosen for the interior of decorator David Mlinaric's house in Somerset. All are rooted in earlier colors found on site. In the bedroom and adjoining dressing room, a blue had been used, and accordingly Mlinaric and his design partner, Hugh Henry, mixed up a related shade of the same color. Unusually they opted for limewash, rather than oil paint or distemper, which gives particular depth of tone. Limewash is rarely used in this context. Normally it is limited to the external walls or service areas of a house, since it cannot be cleaned and easily rubs off, although at an early date it was employed in even the grandest interiors, such as those at Hardwick Hall (pages 52–3). Mlinaric's decision to use it here represents an interesting revival of an old tradition and an unconventional one. Few would take the risk of using a paint with such obvious practical drawbacks. But the deep, luminous color could never have been achieved using any other medium.

INDEX

Figures in *italics* indicate photographs; those in **bold** indicate main entries.

FURTHER READING

This book looks at paint in the context of interior decoration in Great Britain and Ireland and is mainly concerned with the work of a select group of designers. It is not intended as a comprehensive study, but rather as an introduction. For those wishing to explore the subject more fully we would particularly recommend the following sources. Unless otherwise stated, all were published in London.

The most comprehensive and authoritative study of the pre-Victorian period is Ian Bristow's two-volume work, **Architectural Colour in British Interiors 1615–1840** and **Interior House-Painting Colours and Technology 1615–1840** (Yale University Press, 1996), which also contain the fullest published bibliography of relevant primary and secondary sources. We would also draw attention to the articles published by Ian Bristow under the editorship of Malcolm Airs in the "**Great Houses**" series produced by Oxford University Press, namely **The Seventeenth-century Great House** (1995); **The Later Eighteenth Century Great House** (1997); **The Regency Great House** (1998), **The Victorian Great House** (2000); **The Edwardian Great House** (2000). These again contain valuable references to relevant primary and secondary sources. Other useful modern studies include Noël Heaton, **Outlines of Paint Technology** (2nd ed., C. Griffin & Co., 1940), John Stewart Remington and Wilfrid Francis, **Pigments. Their Manufacture, Properties, and Use** (3rd rev. ed., Leonard Hill 1954), and Rosamond Harley, **Artists' Pigments c.1600–1835** (new ed., Butterworths, 1970). We would also recommend the practical guides to historic paint published by both English Heritage and the Society for the Protection of Ancient Buildings.

A wealth of literature exists on the wider subject of interior decoration, among which we would single out such pioneering studies as Margaret Jourdain's **Decoration in England from 1660 to 1770** (Batsford, 1914) and **English Decoration and Furniture of the Later XVIIIth Century (1760–1820)** (Batsford, 1922), as well as more recent works, including John Cornforth, **English Interiors 1790–1848. The Quest for Comfort** (Barrie & Jenkins, 1978), **The Inspiration of the Past. Country House Taste in the Twentieth Century** (Viking, 1985), and, with John Fowler, the landmark publication, **English Interior Decoration in the 18th Century** (Barrie & Jenkins, 1974); Mario Praz, **An Illustrated History of Interior Decoration** (Thames & Hudson, 1964); Peter Thornton, **Seventeenth Century Interior Decoration in England, France and Holland** (Yale University Press, 1978) and **Authentic Decor. The Domestic Interior 1620–1820** (Weidenfeld & Nicolson, 1984); Charles Saumarez Smith, **Eighteenth Century Decoration** (Weidenfeld & Nicolson, 1993); Charlotte Gere, **Nineteenth-Century Decoration** (Weidenfeld & Nicolson, 1989); and Stephen Calloway, **Twentieth-Century Decoration** (Weidenfeld & Nicolson, 1988).

The careers of individual designers are covered in a wide range of publications, including books, articles, and exhibition catalogues. Those consulted in connection with this book include Eileen Harris, **The Genius of Robert Adam. His Interiors** (Yale University Press, 2001); John Harris and Michael Snodin (eds.), **Sir William Chambers. Architect to George III**, exh. cat. (Courtauld Gallery, 1997); Dorothy Stroud, **George Dance, Architect 1741–1825** (Faber & Faber, 1971); Margaret Richardson and Mary Anne Stevens (eds.), **John Soane. Architect**, exh. cat. (Royal Academy, 1999); Megan Aldrich (ed.), **The Craces: Royal Decorators 1768–1899**, exh. cat. (Brighton, 1990); Margaret Richardson, **George Aitchison. Lord Leighton's Architect**, exh. cat. (RIBA, 1980); John Martin Robinson, **The Wyatts. An Architectural Dynasty** (Oxford University Press, 1979); A. S. G. Butler, **The Architecture of Sir Edwin Lutyens**, 3 vols. (Country Life, 1950); Christopher Hussey, **The Work of Sir Robert Lorimer** (Country Life, 1931); Robert Becker, **Nancy Lancaster. Her life, her world, her art** (Alfred A. Kopf, New York, 1996); and David Hicks' own publications, especially **David Hicks on Decoration** (Leslie Frewin, 1966), **David Hicks on Living – with Taste** (Leslie Frewin, 1968), **Living with Design** (Weidenfeld & Nicolson, 1979), and **Style and Design** (Harmondsworth Viking, 1987)

For the history of individual houses and interiors, guide books are a mine of information, and many of the examples we feature have also been covered in articles published in **Country Life** and elsewhere.

To all these various publications we owe a significant debt, which we gratefully acknowledge.

ACKNOWLEDGEMENTS

Thoughts on a book on interior paint and color have been with me for many years. John Sutcliffe, who first taught me to paint and restore, over 25 years ago, has been a key influence. John Cornforth, who for considerably longer has guided the working lives of so many involved in historic interiors, was responsible for my sitting on the staircase leading to David Mlinaric's studio (no desk room deemed appropriate), some 25 years ago, in an attempt to train me for work at the National Trust. I would like to thank many at the National Trust, particularly Christopher Wall and Tony Mitchell, and for valuable advice the Marchioness of Dufferin and Ava, the Hon. Desmond Guinness, the Hon. Marina Guinness, Robert Kime, Chrstopher Moore, and Jeremy Williams. I must also pay tribute to the scholarship of Ian Bristow, whose separate books on painting techniques and the historic use of color have proved invaluable in compiling the present text.

Above all I want to thank the owners and carers of the houses we visited and photographed. For over a month we were made to feel welcome to take photographs by the Duke of Buccleuch & Queensberry KT, the Duke & Duchess of Abercorn, the Marquess of Hertford, the Earl and Countess of Longford, the Earl of Pembroke and Montgomery, the Earl of March and Kinrara, the Earl of Erne, Lord Rothschild, the Knight of Glin, Mrs Caroline Workman and Mrs Zoe England, Bath & N E Somerset Council, the Leeds Castle Foundation, the Kelmarsh Trust, the Trustees of Sir John Soane's Museum, the Sutherland Trust, the Irish Georgian Society and the National Trust.

This book is a Farrow & Ball book and would not have been possible without the company's support and especially that of my friend and business partner, Martin Ephson, and co-directors Sarah Cole and John Hackett. Special and personal thanks to Pamela Power who quite faultlessly planned the 100 or so visits to houses.

As the book drew near to completion thanks to all those involved in its detail, Polly Powell at Cassell Illustrated ,and Deborah Simpson, our graphic designer. Also those who read the book in draft and made crucial comments, especially John Cornforth and Tim Knox of the National Trust.

Finally, no mention has been made of either Ivan Terestchenko, who took the photographs and guided the layout, or Joe Friedman, who helped with the conception and writing of the book. Whatever my role has been, it is these two who, through their friendship and professionalism, have more than any other created the book you see.

Lastly I want to thank my sisters- and brothers-in-law, Rosaleen, Fiona, Finn, Thomasin, and Catriona Guinness at Biddesden and Keiran Guinness at Knockmaroon, and my wife Mirabel for her unfailing support.

Tom Helme
Farrow & Ball